Still Desperate in the PROMISED LAND

DON OGLESBY

The story of Homes of Hope, a South Carolina ministry

Copyright 2021 by Don Oglesby

Edited and Published by BiographyMasters.com

BIOGRAPHY MASTERS

IN PRAISE OF STILL DESPERATE IN THE PROMISED LAND

Some stories will move people to tears. This story moves people off the streets into homes! Teeming with God-glorifying miracles, shrewd business principles and remarkable individuals, the story of Homes of Hope is a must read!

Dr. Peter Hubbard
Teaching Pastor, North Hills Church, Taylors, SC.

This story of Homes of Hope shows them to be a model of innovation, discipline, and love. And also a partner/teacher equipping us to love our neighbors in practical and economically sustainable ways. They are helping us reimagine what is possible through building a loving, redemptive community. The lessons we have learned are transforming how we live out Jesus' calling to biblical community.
    Bill White—Teaching Pastor, Grace Church, Greenville, SC

This book is a powerful testament to how a leader like Don Oglesby, and his colleagues, can impact the lives of the poor when they listen to the voice of God, answer God's call, and remain faithful to their purpose despite the struggles. By following their path, God gave them favor and they succeeded in their mission far beyond their expectations. During a time of so many false narratives about the quick and easy path to success, this story highlights the simple truth about God's plan for humanity; Love the Lord your God...Love your neighbor... If we do that, everything else will fall into place. Thank you for sharing your journey and such a powerful story about purpose.

Bernie Mazyck—President/CEO—SC Association for Community and Economic Development

I am pleased to endorse Still Desperate in the Promised Land. I was watching as God berthed this ministry. It was clear that Don, Bob and the other early ministry leaders had a heart for Christ and a passion for the cause. I saw the sacrifices they made personally as they committed to follow God in launching this ministry, regardless of the personal cost. Miracle Hill has been pleased to partner with Homes of Hope since their inception. I celebrate the great way God has used them. And I am blessed by the key spiritual lessons they have learned and now share with others. God is at work at Homes of Hope!

Reid Lehman—Former President/CEO—Miracle Hill Ministries— Greenville, SC

Don's story of his Homes of Hope journey is a celebration of community and personal rejuvenation, creatively told with deep understanding and compassion.

Russell Stall—City Councilman—City of Greenville, SC

THIS BOOK IS DEDICATED TO:

All of the families and individuals who have been served in some way by Homes of Hope. You are the reason God called Homes of Hope into existence. It is all for you. You have inspired us, and continue to inspire us. Thank you for trusting us in your faith and success journeys.

Current staff and former staff of Homes of Hope—your commitment and passion, your love and compassion, and your own sense of calling in your own lives, together with being my family for over twenty years, has inspired me. You are the ones who have served on the front lines. Sometimes bullets fly by your heads, but you keep advancing. The definition of a hero is someone who puts others above themselves in the face of danger. You are heroes.

The Solid Rock Club—your faithfulness to give monthly over all these years inspires each of us. We truly see you as foundational, like the Bible story of solid rock versus sinking sand. We love you. Lives have been changed because of you.

All donors of capital, materials, time volunteering, advocating and consulting over the years—we simply would not be here without you, but more importantly the families and individuals we've served would not have been served. Lives have been changed because of you.

All of the cities, counties, municipalities, councils of government, units of government, as well as state and federal government—your passions for the people you serve in affordable housing is evident, and without your funds the number of people we've served would be less than half of what they are.

My mother, Ruth Cooper Oglesby—you taught me and my brother Gary, in the middle of the 1960's in Alabama, how to unconditionally love everyone, regardless of their skin color or anything else that might have made them different from me. I will always be grateful to you that you had the courage to take that stance among your friends and family, and teach it to us, your boys.

FOREWORD

I'll never forget first meeting Don Oglesby.

Spring, 2009 – the U.S. was in the deepest trough of the worst economic crisis since The Great Depression. Naively, I was starting a business.

I was assembling a group of CEOs willing to pay about $1,000 monthly to become part of an informal board of advisors. Fellow leaders that would serve each other, telling them what they really needed to hear, even if they didn't want to hear it. Peers that would help them become better leaders, who made better decisions, and got better results. I would be their convener, their confidant, their 'Chair.' I would facilitate their monthly workshops; bring them expert speakers; and serve each one, individually, as their executive coach.

I needed eight *Yes'* to launch. After months of training and trying, I had only one. I also had a huge number of *No's,* most accompanied by colorful language asserting I was insane to even ask given current economic times. I went from one disappointing conversation to the next. I was beginning to wonder what in the world I was doing, even though I knew God had called me to do so.

One morning that spring, I sat across the breakfast table from a most unusual, yet very common, everyman. Don Oglesby led an organization called Homes of Hope. I wanted at least one not-for-profit organization on my board. When it came to impactful non-profits making a huge difference in the community, Homes of Hope was 'the real deal.' They had already built a reputation for developing fiscally responsible housing projects that made our hometown of Greenville, SC a better place to be and live. So, I thought I knew them before we even sat down. I was wrong.

Don and I hit it off immediately. Until then, I had met very few CEOs and leaders who regularly and clearly heard the voice of the Lord. But it was clear from our initial conversation that an ongoing, two-way dialogue, with our creator was a routine part of Don's everyday life. Clearly, this man walked closely with God.

To my delight, Don was interested in the vision I was selling. But, when he heard I was recruiting only CEOs for the Board, he told me he wasn't qualified since he didn't hold that position at Homes of Hope.

Before I could express my confusion, Don saw the look on my face and clarified:

> "I'm just the President. God is the CEO. Always has been. Always will be."

I nodded slowly, trying to grasp more fully this important distinction. I kind of got it, but I wanted to know more about what that meant to Don. Unprompted, he continued:

> "Now, if it helps, I do have a weekly meeting with the CEO. Every Wednesday at 8:30 AM, I sit with a blank pad of paper and a pen. I listen for God's voice and take notes about anything and everything He wants me to know about Homes of Hope, and how He wants me to lead it."

> "How long do those meetings last?" I asked.

> "Usually about two hours, but sometimes longer if He's got a lot to say, or if I'm slow to understand His meaning, which is usually the case," Don replied.

Wow. This guy was clearly serious about this CEO/President distinction thing, and about his dependence upon God's guidance to lead! Personally, I don't think I'd ever spent 2 hours silently in God's presence listening and waiting for Him to download a message. Don did it every week!

> "What a blessing it would be to have Don on my Board," I thought.

I was sold! I wanted Homes of Hope. I wanted Don as a member of the Board. So I told him I'd happily make an exception in his case and we'd allow a 'mere President' to fill a seat on the board. (Who was I kidding? I had one member and needed seven more!)

Don was thankful for my generous accommodation, but then added that, as much as he wanted to join, the membership fee just wasn't in the budget. Now, this objection was vastly more familiar to me. I'd heard it dozens of times over the prior few months. But as I heard it from Don that day, I also clearly heard the Lord say:

> 'Ask him, to ask me, for the money.'

I paused for just a moment to take than in. Then quickly, I blurted out:

> "Why don't you ask God to provide the money for the group? How about we touch base in a week? If you unexpectedly receive a gift that covers the first year's membership dues, take it as a sign that you've heard from Him. If not, take that as a sign as well. Sound good?"

Don loved the idea and agreed immediately. We prayed together and asked God to provide exactly that degree of clarity.

It didn't take a week. Two days later Don called and said that the hoped-for unexpected funding came through – he was 'in.' My heart leapt for joy!

Eight more members quickly followed. The next month, eleven of us began our journey together as the Peer Advisory Board I knew God called me to form. Our Board was off and running and I had found in Don Oglesby a friend who would ultimately become closer than a brother.

A couple of years later, God used Don in my life in another powerful way. One morning I was reflecting with gratitude upon all the times over the prior decade God had spoken to me so clearly. I noticed a theme, and asked God about it:

> *"Lord, why does it seem that every time you speak to me so clearly, it's always about something that deeply impacts me, my family, my career, or my business?"*

I didn't like the answer.

> *"Brett, I'm just speaking to you about the things you care about."*

Ouch!

God's revelation of the obvious self-centeredness of my prayer life landed on me with a thud in my heart. I literally fell to the floor of my office, face down, and wept, feeling the weight of the truth He had just spoken to me. God did a deep work in me in the moments that followed.

Eventually, as God's righteous conviction completed its work in me, I acknowledged, and apologized, for my selfish approach to my prayers. Then I asked God another question:

> *"Father, thank you for your forgiveness. Could you give me a clear word about someone else; For someone other than me that you'd like to bless through me?"*

Immediately I heard:

> *"Could I?"*

Ha! God has always been great at calling me out on the unbelief I express through my poor choice of words! I chuckled to myself at His witty reply and quickly corrected the phrasing of my request:

> *"Sorry Father. Yes, of course you can! You created the universe and all that's in it ... out of nothing! Of course, you can certainly handle this simple request. I KNOW you can. But will you? Lord, will you please speak something to me you'd like me to share with someone else? Anyone else?"*

His reply came immediately as the computer up on my desk sprang to life. It made an audible noise signaling that I had just received an email. Then I heard this from the Lord:

> *"That email, the one that just arrived, is for Don Oglesby. Send it to him."*

Excitedly, I jumped up from the floor, went to the desk, and read the new email waiting in my Inbox. Curiously, the message contained a Bible verse. But, I didn't see any relevance to issues or opportunities I knew Don was dealing with at the time. I was a bit confused. I paused for just a moment, thinking I might have heard God wrong. But immediately I got the confirmation:

> *"Send it to him now Brett. Right now."*

Reencouraged, I forwarded the message to Don, along with a brief message of explanation – something like:

> *"Don, I'm not sure how, but I have a strong sense that this verse is for you today."*

Less than five minutes later, I received Don's reply:

> *"Wow, Brett. That verse contained exactly the message I've been praying about for a long time. It's personal. Deeply personal to me. So much so, that I may never be able to give you all the context about what it means to*

me. But I want to assure you that you clearly heard from the Lord on this. Thanks for sending it to me."

Such is one of many of the ways God regularly uses Don Oglesby in the lives of others. Don is always longing for, and listening to, the voice of his heavenly Father. Don's always encouraging others in their own walks of faith. Don's way of being, and leading, in the world seems to work.

Since its inception in 1998, Homes of Hope has:

- Developed nearly 700 homes across the State of South Carolina;

- Impacted thousands of families, 10s of thousands of individual lives;

- Restored the lives over 300 men recovering from addiction, giving them the skills, training, and faith, they need to become the productive contributing members of society God created them to be;

- Employed over 50 employees. Not just providing them with paychecks, health insurance, and benefits needed to support their families. But inspiring them with assurance they're serving causes greater than themselves that truly matter to humanity;

- Engaged with over 2000 volunteers allowing them to participate in those same causes;

- Maintained a consistently healthy P&L Statement, and a Balance Sheet that's the envy of any for-profit business (and makes all bankers and lenders salivate!);

- Enrolled hundreds of individual and corporate financial donors – enabling them to co-create these profound differences in the world while simultaneously providing them the opportunity to partner with an entrepreneurial not-for-profit that doesn't *need* their support, but knows that

God calls them to ask for it so that they too can be blessed by the work He is doing through them (How cool is that?).

Homes of Hope has been consistently successful, in good economic times and in horrible economic times. They've NEVER had a down year! How is that even possible?

Simple. Yet so difficult. By the grace of God, under Don's leadership, Homes of Hope has learned the secret that most of us never fully grasp:

> **How to remain just as desperate for God's vision, direction, correction, favor, and provision in the Promised Land, as we were when we wandered through our own wilderness years.**

The book you hold in your hand can teach you that secret. It contains stories empowered by powerful truths. Not heady, conceptual truths that sound good in theory but have no practical application. But hard-hitting, heaven-down-to-earth, practical truths revealed and discovered in the crucible of life's experiences. Useful truths that can transform lives – can transform YOUR LIFE – if you take them to heart and apply them in your everyday moments.

As you'll read in this book, you'll discover that Don has a very novel way of viewing his relationship with God. Don believes he's not only just one of God's beloved children; Don believes he's actually God's favorite child!

He doesn't just say that. Don really, down to his core, believes it to be true. Of course, he's quick to add:

"I'm tied for 1st ... with you!"

How might you live and lead differently; what might you be able to accomplish, if you knew, and truly believed that you were the favorite child of the benevolent creator of the universe, who loves you immeasurably more than you could ever ask or imagine, and desires to give good gifts to you?

Read this book and allow God to speak to you personally. Let Him unpack these truths, and reveal fresh truths, for you too!

You're about to meet Don Oglesby. I've built him up in this foreword and I know Don hates that I've done so. But know this:

> Don Oglesby is just an ordinary man.

BUT, Don knows he's loved by *Extraordinary* God. A God who trusts him to lead an impactful ministry and run a successful business – from God's agenda, in God's ways, for God's purposes.

Turn the page. Allow Don's stories, and most especially God's love, to penetrate your heart and your being. I promise you this: You'll be glad that you did, and you'll never forget the meeting.

Brett Pyle

CEO Coach
Transformational Speaker
Author – *Your Extraordinary Why, Living a Successful Life of Significance (2020)*

INTRODUCTION

Our story began with six people who felt a calling to serve God. The fact that a sole benefactor paid for it all, might have given confidence that the calling was real.

Those same six were shaken to the core though, one particular day in late 2000, and they didn't know what to do. This all happened in the few seconds that it took to say "We don't have any support anymore." But in those same few seconds, they all collectively proclaimed, "We will trust God."

This is the story of a faith journey. The faith journey of Homes of Hope; A ministry in South Carolina whose mission is to "Open doors for economic mobility through housing, economic, and workforce development."

Everyone reading this has a journey. We all have either had great leaps of faith or great lacks of faith over our lifetimes.

Our journey began that day.

It obviously was a journey that we didn't expect, for we thought our destination was already at hand. But in time it was a journey that taught us so much more than we'd ever imagined. It taught us how to live in the destination of calling once we arrived. It was a journey which, if not taken, would have yielded a much different ending.

It was also a journey that connected us.

We had no idea then, because the wilderness we walked through was so hard, we often didn't pause long enough to see what we were being taught. But the connections to those we served, and would serve in the future, were immeasurable. We only had "an idea" of what it was like to struggle for survival when your circumstances were difficult, or when barriers to success in life were too great to hurdle.

But after walking through the wilderness, we knew. At least in part. We knew what that felt like, as best that we could know, and how the obstacles faced by those we served were profound, real, challenging, and tiresome.

It is my hope that by reading about this journey, you will find places in your own heart, your mind, and your life, to enhance your own faith journey. And while the stories and principles in this book were learned by those who went through that journey, I hope that some of them will spark something in each of you. In the unique ways that only God can use, it is possible that you are the objects of His teaching as you read this.

Maybe this story was meant to show an example of God's faithfulness and His willingness to do whatever it took for a group who trusted Him, to empower them to fulfill His calling. Or, maybe He will indeed give you some of our story to be a small template in your life. That is up to Him, and how you receive these things. Either way, I am happy if something within these pages produces life within your own journey.

In this book, you will read about our wilderness. Where we learned the difference between trust and faith. You will also read about how He called us out of the desert into a place where He intended for us to flourish. You will read about the lessons we learned, the ground we worked, and the desperation that tied it all together each day.

And if you're reading this via the glasses of a non-profit leader or ministry leader, it is my hope that you will also be interested in the execution of our mission and how the methods we use have continually tied-back to our journey experiences, and what God had taught us.

For whatever reason you are reading this, my hope is that being "still desperate in the promised land" will become real to you, and you will understand the great freedom this concept brings. It was life changing for us.

I am grateful you're giving this book your time. It has been a dream to write this for almost 2 decades, and it is my hope and prayer that it will be of benefit to you.

Table Of Contents

FOREWORD 7

INTRODUCTION...15

PART I
FOUNDING PRINCIPLES 20

IN THE BEGINNING.. 21

    1   BUS STATION FAITH...22
    2   GOD WILL ALWAYS PAY FOR IT 26
    3   THE FAVOR PRINCIPLE...................................... 30

WALKING IN THE WILDERNESS 36

    4   REALLY HARD, REALLY LIBERATING 37
    5   CRYING AT THE WINDOW................................. 44
    6   REST IN THE MIDST OF THE BUSY-NESS........... 50
    7   THE 9/11 LADY..56
    8   THE WILDERNESS GROUP..................................59
    9   WE'RE ALL JUST GUESSING 65
    10 THE FAMILY PRINCIPLE 68

CROSSING THE JORDAN 73

    11 VISIBILITY LEADS TO CREDIBILITY 74
    12 THE MOVE TO GREENVILLE................................79

PART II
OPERATING FROM CALLING 84

THE PROMISED LAND 85

1. DON'T BE AFRAID 86
2. EMBRACING THE FAITH ADVENTURE 92
3. THE FOCUS IS ON LIVES, NOT NUMBERS 100
4. BEING STRATEGIC 105
5. MEN'S WORKFORCE DEVELOPMENT 116

WORKING MORE FERTILE LAND 124

6. CULTURE SHIFTS AND CORPORATE BONES.. 125
7. BALANCE OF COMMUNITY AND ECONOMIC DEVELOPMENT 128
8. INNOVATION IN FINANCE 133

PART III
FINISH WELL AND PASS THE BATON 137

STILL DESPERATE 138

9. THE POOR ARE WITH YOU................................139
10. RENEWED FAITH, RENEWED FIGHT.................145
11. EVEN MORE DESPERATE 150

ACKNOWLEDGEMENTS 152

AFTERWORD 156

PART I

FOUNDING PRINCIPLES

PART I is our story of passion and why we endured the wilderness, and how our sense of calling compelled us to trust Him even when the evidence was not there.

It is our hope that the founding principles that emerged from the wilderness would be encouraging for the reader, and that many of these principles would become part of each of your own calling in life.

IN THE BEGINNING

BUS STATION FAITH

"In you, Lord my God, I put my trust"
Psalm 25:1

The faith journey started when I read a book about a man I'd never heard of, written by an author I'd never heard of. It was titled "Rees Howells, Intercessor" and I felt strangely compelled to read it.

Reading had never come easy for me. In fact, the reality was that it took me forever to read a book. I am the kind that has to have complete focus when reading or I can't comprehend what I'm reading, so I just did not read very often.

But Howells' book captivated me like no other had before, except for the Bible. I was under its spell quickly because it talked of the one thing I hungered for more than any other at the time—how to live a Spirit-led life.

One of the stories was about Howells needing to travel a good distance to take care of his dying mother but having no money to make the trip. He prayed, and felt God indeed leading him to go. So, he packed his bags, left his home, and got in line at the bus station to purchase a ticket to the town where his mother lived. Only, he had no money.

Here's the part that changed my life, like nothing outside of scripture ever had before, or ever would. He stood in line with the utter and complete expectation that God would send someone who would provide the money for the ticket. And God did.

Just before he reached the ticket window, a man completely unfamiliar to Howells stepped up and said something like "I don't know who you are, but I feel that God is telling me to give you this money....so here." Shoving the money in his hand, he turned and walked away. And of course, it was enough to purchase the ticket.

I didn't know it then, but my life changed that day. Not in a harvest sort of way, but in a seed sort of way.

My Spirit leapt, but my feet stayed on the ground.

Most of us who have and practice faith, might think lofty thoughts of ourselves if we stayed in our prayer closets that day praying for money to purchase a bus ticket, when God confirmed He was calling us to visit our mothers in another town. We would stay there praying because we believed. We knew God was able and we expected Him to answer.

But did we really?

Did we really expect God to answer when we were still at home in the closet?

I'd never thought of my faith as small or weak; not at all. In fact, I would have told you I had big, strong faith. But in reality, what I had was big, strong *dead* faith.

James said, "Faith without works is dead." I always thought that meant our faith was no good if we just kept to ourselves. Preachers told me this all my life, "Get out and love people, and help the least of these." We needed to show our faith by what we did.

But "upon further review" (like the referee always says on an instant replay in football), you learn that the Greek word for "works" in that passage means more than just doing something. The definition also includes one of "activation."

Think about a machine at rest. It might be big, and it might be strong, but unless you plug it into the wall socket for power, what you have is a big, strong dead machine. It's of no use if un-activated.

Faith without activation is dead.

So what does that mean? It means that anyone can have faith to believe. But God wants us to trust. Believing means we are sure that God can. Trusting means we are sure that God will.

Active faith, yes, Bus Station faith is the kind that risks looking like an idiot if God doesn't come through. Howells would have looked foolish if he made it to the ticket window with no money. But he trusted. He knew that God would. We stay in our prayer closets believing God can. Howells got in line.

Then my seed burst forth.

I was called to lead Homes of Hope about a year after it was birthed. It was, and is, my life's calling. It is one of the reasons I was born.

Homes of Hope was born in 1998 through the inspired vision of its founder, Tim Revis. Tim was so inspired that he completely funded the work through his business. But a little more than a year later, and just a few months after I was called there, the down turning economy seized a victim. Tim had to sell his business and could not fund the ministry of Homes of Hope any longer. He fought the inevitable for a long time without sharing the pending doom with us, because his persistent optimism wouldn't let him think anything other than the fact that God would show him a way.

But God had something else in mind. Tim reached the point of no return and called me to have lunch one November day at Atha's Restaurant. There, he said the words that could have stung like a scorpion. He said, "I can't give Homes of Hope any more money. What are you going to do?"

The next words out of my mouth were the most confidently unsure words I'd ever spoken. "We're going to trust God."

And my harvest began.

What followed was a brief staff meeting with me and the 5 employees, who oversaw with me the work of Homes of Hope and its $400,000 annual budget. In the meeting I recounted the story of my lunch with Tim and what he asked me. "What did you say?" they asked. "I said we're going to trust God."

Well, they all knew what that meant.

They looked at each other, then at me, then back at each other, and almost simultaneously (like all those white robed people in Revelation, who always seem to say everything in unison) "Well, we are too," they said.

And we did. We got in line. We literally acted like the money was still there and we went back to work. Oh, but we had a long road ahead of us. To go from $400,000 in support to zero in one day, was...well...there were no words.

What followed was two years of what we call our "Wilderness time," and it was dry, hot and barren. But we did the most crucial part that day, and continue it to this day; we got in the bus ticket line.

Faith is believing God can, trust is believing He will. We risked looking like idiots if God didn't come through. We activated our Bus Station Faith that day and every day thereafter.

It was the closest to a great thing that I ever did.

GOD WILL ALWAYS PAY FOR IT

"Peter replied, 'Lord if it's you, tell me to come to you....'"
Matthew 14:28

In "Bus Station Faith," I described the first of our three original founding principles learned at Homes of Hope which is-Faith. The second principle is Focus.

One day during our wilderness period, I got the bright idea to call a meeting of our team and lay out the roadmap to the Promised Land. To us, the Promised Land meant no more working for free and a sustainable financial support model in place. I thought, *If I'm the one called to lead, it is up to me to hear from God and know how He wants to lead us out of this wilderness.*

Good thinking, huh?

So, I bought some poster boards and Sharpie pens and proceeded to chart income, expenses, programs, procedures, and policies. Well, it was quite the display when I got done.

The Bible says to write out your vision and make it plain, right?

I admired my workmanship and called in the team. They were kind to me as I explained this wonderful plan and although they were supportive, it didn't go like I had hoped.

I can't recall how I ended the meeting, but I do remember it was awkward. During the meeting I was sure that I had missed the target, and that God wasn't pleased with my attempt. I also remember the feeling I had of extreme frustration.

About a week later, my friend Winn Freeman, who has since passed on, called and said, "Let's go see Jimmy Jones."

Winn knew of our wilderness experiences because we talked often, but also because his ministry, Wisdom in Living Life, was going through its own wilderness. He was a great friend during that time, and we learned and grew together.

But that day, I wasn't in the mood to go see anyone named Jimmy Jones whom I'd never heard of. I had my own problems. I had failed to hear from the Lord for specific direction and I'd looked like a poor leader to my team. In fact, a few days after that meeting, while I was praying and seeking His direction and trying to figure out what happened to my poster-board plans, I heard Him speak to me, as clearly as He'd ever done before, or since. He said, "Will you quit trying to make me fit on a spreadsheet?"

Wow. That was one of those moments a person never forgets. Not only did I hear from God, but what I heard made me feel pretty small and unspiritual, even though He said it with great love.

Still, Winn wanted me to go see Jimmy Jones.

"Who's he?" I asked.

"He runs a ministry in Columbia, South Carolina, totally on faith," said Winn. "He 'prays in' all of his support. Runs it all with volunteers. He's an amazing guy. I think he can help us."

Well, clearly I didn't know what I was doing, so I said, "Sure."

On the drive to his office, I remember looking out the passenger window wondering about what to do with this ministry I was so passionate about. Was it real? Did God really call us? If He did, why was it so hard? Why wasn't He sending an abundance of support? Why did we always have to wait until the office water service was about to be cut off before having the money to pay the bill?

I remember silently praying, "Lord, I really don't want to go to Columbia today. I could be doing so many other things to help Homes of Hope be what you called it to be. I feel like I'm wasting my time. Lord, would you please make sure I don't waste my time today, and would you please speak to me through this man, whoever he is?"

I didn't hear an answer then, but boy, did I get one when I met Jimmy!

When we arrived, Winn made the introductions and Jimmy graciously gave us a tour of his ministry facilities. He was not an impressive looking man—even a bit awkward one might say. Later, I was reminded that many looked at Christ in the same way. But as he spoke and shared his heart, I saw that underneath, he displayed a closeness and intimacy with the Father that I've only witnessed in a handful of others over my lifetime.

Casually almost, Jimmy wove stories and principles that he'd learned into our tour. Everything he said was seasoned with scripture and personal stories of answers to prayer. To this day, I can remember almost all of them. I have repeated most of them so often that I have to remind myself that I didn't hear them in a burning bush, but in fact borrowed them from Jimmy.

There was one life changing word he said that day that stuck with me the most. It became our second founding principle—focus.

After spending an hour with Jimmy, he finally asked, "Don, how many houses per year do you want Homes of Hope to build?" I puffed out my chest and said "Fifty houses per year is our goal."

He replied, "Well, what if the Lord only wanted you to build five? What would happen?"

I said, "Umm……uh…."

He said, "I'll tell you what would happen. At the end of that year, you'd build your fifty homes, but when the bill came due, the Lord would only hand you the money for five, and He'd hand you the bill for forty-five."

I was stunned. He was right.

He said, "Don, always focus on exactly what the Lord called you to do, and He will always pay for it."

I never forgot that.

It becomes so easy for us to run ahead of God, especially if we want to do something really badly and we HOPE He chooses to come along with us. But the hard thing, and the thing that I see many other ministries and people do, even when we are sure of the call, is that sometimes we stop listening to His voice.

I knew God called us to build houses for low-income families. But I thought it was okay to build fifty of them per year. The truth was I didn't know how many He wanted us to build.

The important thing wasn't determining the correct number though! The important thing was staying in tune with His voice and focusing on His calling.

The principle of Focus compels us to know what God is saying at all times. And, it compels us to stay true to it, and not presume that He's okay with your big idea just because it seems to go along with what He's said already.

I tried to chart our way out of the wilderness and find a spreadsheet that would fit God and lead us to sustainability. The truth is that God is *the* source, not a resource. He won't fit on a spreadsheet, and He wants us to focus on what He called us to do.

And if we do, I promise you, He will always pay for it. He always has.

THE FAVOR PRINCIPLE
He never rains down plants

"So, neither the one who plants nor the one who waters is anything, but only God, who makes things grow."

1 Corinthians 3:7-8

The third learned principle at Homes of Hope is like the first two in that each, when examined alone, could be seen as the most important of the three. The third principle is God's FAVOR. It is life-changing.

In March of 2003 the Lord spoke to us and said, "It's time for Homes of Hope to cross the Jordan and enter the Promised Land of my calling." I had an idea what He meant. We had been in the wilderness for quite some time (over 2 years). Working for free and acting like the money was there while we fulfilled our calling, was the most profound experience I'd ever gone through. I tell folks today that it is the "steel that strengthened us." I wouldn't trade it for anything in the world.

But wilderness living can be tiresome. The whole time you're there, you're wandering, looking for the Promised Land. God saying, "Cross the Jordan now," was what we longed to hear! I felt led to re-read the book of Joshua and to remember the story of the Israelites when they crossed the Jordan. When finished, I gathered everybody by calling a meeting and began to explain to them what I felt the Lord was teaching us in the midst of that. What He taught us became our third founding principle, needing God's favor. How do you get it from Him? What does it look like? Who qualifies for God's favor?

I'd like to share with you what He taught us.

But first, I want to share a type of paradox for you to ponder. This is taken from the scripture above.

Here's the paradox:

YOU CAN'T GET GOD'S FAVOR BY PLANTING AND WATERING

but....

YOU CAN'T GET GOD'S FAVOR UNLESS YOU PLANT AND WATER

In 1992, Clint Eastwood directed and starred in a movie called "Unforgiven." Near the end of the movie, as he is about to kill Gene Hackman, or at least his character, Gene Hackman says, "I don't deserve to die like this." Just before Clint Eastwood shoots him, he says, "Deserve has got nothing to do with it."

Lesson #1 in learning the principle of God's favor, "deserve" has nothing to do with it."

> The primary reason God calls you, is because you can't do it. As the scripture states: John 15:5: *"Apart from Me, you can do nothing."*

In relation to His calling, God gives His favor for one reason; because we need it. Not because we deserve it, or have earned it, but because we need it.

Planting and watering are the things we do, but they grow only because of God's favor. He doesn't give favor because we planted and watered. That would mean we earned it, or even deserved it. Maybe we did work hard, and some would say we earned it or deserved it. But that's not relevant.

He gives favor because we need it. "Apart from me, you can do nothing."

In Bible College I learned to "study-out" a lot of words in scripture to determine their more in-depth meanings, because often-times the English language wasn't sufficient compared to the Greek or Hebrew words used.

When you study-out the Greek definition of the word used in the above scripture for "nothing," you find that it means, well, nothing.

Now, you could stop here and say you have learned the principle of favor; that it is all up to God. We need Him and our works don't save us, but you would fall short of full understanding if you did.

The second part of the paradox above contains the truth of:

Lesson #2 in learning the principle of God's favor: If you don't plant and water there is nothing for God to make grow.

In the wilderness we were desperate for God to rain-down manna from heaven every day because the wilderness is a desert! When I remember our time there, I picture us sitting with our legs crossed and arms outstretched, waiting for food. There was no fertile dirt to work.

In the Promised Land, there is fertile ground, and seeds in abundance, but we still must look to the manna-maker to cause our seeds to grow into plants. The biggest difference is that in the desert it was all up to Him. In the Promised Land, we have to do our part which is planting and watering. In either situation, God's favor has nothing to do with our earning or deserving, we must still be just as desperate for Him in the Promised Land as we were in the wilderness.

In the Promised Land, nothing "rains down" on us like it did when the daily dose of manna fell in the desert. He gives us the fertile land, and seeds, and gives us favor for the growth of our plants, but he never "rains down" plants. We have to plant the seeds, and water them, to receive His growth and His favor.

For Homes of Hope, this translated into identifying what our seeds were; it was housing. He said, "Work the land I've given you." He gave us a product (housing) that fulfilled our mission and calling, but also produces income. Today we produce 70% of our budget needs through housing income.

I'll never forget the first time that happened for us. We had people encouraging us to apply for federal grants to build housing. Until then, we had only rehabbed mobile homes for families in poverty, and sold them for $5,000, which were paid for through $100 per month payments. To me, thinking of applying for federal grants was like thinking of ways to go to the moon using only a pogo stick.

But we did apply, and we were approved for the grant. We built our first ten homes using federal grants. Then the city gave us the land to build on, and money to build a new road.! We never dreamed of being road builders. Frankly, we never dreamed of any of that.

But God made our plants grow, after we planted our seeds and watered them.

YOU CAN'T GET GOD'S FAVOR BY PLANTING AND WATERING

but....

YOU CAN'T GET GOD'S FAVOR UNLESS YOU PLANT AND WATER

He doesn't make the plants grow (favor) as a reward for your hard work. But He does make your plants grow (favor) because you can't make them grow by yourself! And he won't make them grow if they stay in the seed package.

Lastly, who is this principle for?

Lesson #3 in learning the principle of God's favor: This principle is for those experiencing God's calling.

This is important to note. My understanding of the favor principle we were taught, is that this particular definition of the word "favor" is limited in application to a calling from God. This is not favor like, "And Noah found favor with God." Neither is it grace in any form. In the broad range of definitions of the word "favor," like the one I'm talking about here, it is most accurately defined as "support" or "empowerment." In fact, I can't make a good case of this principle being true in many other situations. Not while walking the dog, or taking out the trash, or even helping a poor man on the street corner. I can say though, that it is absolutely true when applied to His specific calling.

All who follow Christ are called at the most basic level to fulfill Matthew 25 and Matthew 28 which is to help folks in need, and go make disciples. This principle applies to that calling too and also has profound implications when applied to specific callings beyond Matthew 25 and 28.

Let's examine a calling for a minute. In the story about the disciples seeing Jesus walk on the water towards their boat, Peter cried out, *"Lord, if it's you, command me to come."* (Matthew 14:28)

"Come," the Lord said. He called him. And the result was the second person in history who walked on water. Now, I know he didn't walk long, but that's not important. Walk he did. Even when he sank, the Lord was quick to grab hold, and pull him back up.

God's calling, when carried out, causes us to walk on water too. The principle of God's favor is for those He calls.

I think that many who struggle with their calling, or many who wonder why their calling seems to keep them stuck in the wilderness, could benefit from the favor principle. I see ministries and individuals sitting in the desert with their figurative legs crossed and their arms outstretched all the time. I wonder if their Promised Land is just over the hill, with fertile dirt and an abundance of seeds. I also see ministries and individuals continually wondering why God's favor isn't given even though they "obey enough." They "deserve it" they rationalize, and blame God for not making plants grow from seed packages, even though the seeds remain in their packages.

Take your seeds out of the package. Find the fertile dirt of your calling. Plant and water your seeds. But above all, be just as desperate for God in the Promised Land as you were in the wilderness. His favor makes it all grow. You need it. He'll give it.

WALKING IN THE WILDERNESS

REALLY HARD, REALLY LIBERATING

"Now, the Lord is the Spirit, and where the Spirit of the Lord is, there is freedom."

2 Corinthians 3:17

Living and working in the wilderness was "interesting." I put "interesting" in quotation marks because we used to say it whenever we couldn't think of a good word to use about a hard situation.

It was hard; there is no doubt about that. But it was liberating too. And none of us would trade having walked through it for anything.

Of the six of us, everyone but me had spouses who were employed. So, while the other five were only paid a Homes of Hope paycheck sporadically during that time, they did have the benefit of some family income. Most weeks, we literally voted on who got a paycheck because we only had raised enough money for one person to be paid. My wife was not employed, as we had decided years before we would try to make it on my income so she could be home with our daughters during their school years.

Our household had $300 in the bank on that fateful day when our wilderness journey began, and now suddenly no income. I was not aware of the financial details of the others in the group or their situations.

But God provided. In the Bible it talks about forty-years of wandering for His chosen people and it talks about how God provided by dropping manna down each day. Similar to that, He continued that for us.

Remember in this story, our predicament regarding support. On day-one of the wilderness journey, our benefactor's funding ceased, and we had no other resources to fall back on. None.

No donors to call. No grants to write. No local foundations that knew us or our work, or anywhere to ask for help. No corporate giving relationships. Nothing.

If you aren't sure that "put all your eggs in one basket" is a bad plan, I assure you, it is indeed a bad plan.

I can't thoroughly explain all of the details of how God provided. Much of it happened unbeknownst to me. How He provided for the other five or Homes of Hope corporately, never fit a distinct pattern. Often it was not seen by everyone at the same time. And I'll admit that some of it escapes my memory.

I know that may seem odd. I can only explain that the wilderness was often a blur. Our mindset during that time was not focused on what He did to provide, but rather focused on the One who provided.

At times, it was as if we were living in a dream world. We couldn't really believe we were still there working without our benefactor's money, and sometimes the things we saw didn't add up to the things that happened.

What I mean is that we knew He did provide for us, but the specific details of His provision seemed less than our actual need. Nevertheless, somehow the books always balanced, the bills always got paid however slowly at times, and we were still there working.

The best part of this fuzziness of specific memories is that we keenly remember the love that we felt collectively from our Father. We also remember how closely knit we were as brothers and sisters trusting our Daddy and fulfilling our collective calling.

I may be a bit inadequate explaining all the ways God provided but I can definitely say He did. Every time Homes of Hope faced a bill we had to pay, something would happen at the last minute to rescue us. Someone would hear about our faith journey and drop by a check. Or, a church would invite us to tell our story, taking up an offering afterwards. Other times someone would purchase a set of handrails from us, or ask us to build a set of steps or a handicapped ramp and offer to pay for it.

Most of our vendors were patient in working with us, although some were a bit less gracious. Unlike our current water company, the water company at that time was on the less gracious list. While other vendors would send us a second invoice or call to discuss, this company simply showed up after five days of being past due , to turn off the water. We began to know our water meter guy pretty well. Somehow, we always managed to send him back with enough money to keep it on.

In the wilderness, you appreciate water a lot.

We also opened a thrift store which turned out to be quite an adventure. We worked like dogs with the intent to make that store financially successful which did not really happen. However, we did find unexpected success in forging and deepening customer relationships, and by offering the community affordable clothing and other items.

The team that ran the store was a special group, led by Pat Odom, who had a vast amount of experience running thrift stores for another ministry. She made the store a ministry on day-one. As far as the team was concerned, caring for others didn't need to be in a mission statement. That came through the eyes, minds and hearts of the staff, and was demonstrated in numerous ways.

They took time getting to know their local customers and sometimes set aside special items they knew they would like for their next trip in. The staff also took time to earnestly listen to them and would stop to pray with them when needed.

The staff was a special group, and the loyal customers were too. We miss them all.

In terms of a strong balance sheet, and profitability, the store was not so successful.

But what it did do for us, was to create something that every entrepreneur and small business owner understands, the importance of creating cash flow.

Many times, while the store was not profitable, it still provided the daily cash deposits that we needed to make it through. It was a lot of work, and for that reason, it was worth it.

So, from the beginning of the wilderness, I declared to the others that as the leader, I would not take a paycheck until the six of us could get one regularly each week. I'm reminded even now, in thinking back on that day, of two prior experiences, that are relevant to that declaration.

My training in business prior to this moment included training in sales. The one thing that stayed consistent in almost all of the sales trainings that I participated in, was that "Once you have the customer convinced, stop talking." It is a principal that still holds true today.

The second experience was something that frequently happened to me in times of worship, particularly while singing in a congregation. There were often times when the words of a particular song just rang so true to me in the moment, that I would be overcome by joy and gratitude for how much God loves His children, and I would choke-up and not be able to sing anymore. I would stop and just bask in the emotion of the moment.

Both things remind me of the thought that I had that day—the day I made the "no paycheck" declaration. The thought is based in Psalm 23. Everyone knows it. It is the most familiar of all the Psalms, maybe of all scripture.

My thought was based on the opening line to Psalm 23; "The Lord is my Shephard, I lack nothing." (New International Version/NIV)

There are times when I know in my spirit that the Lord can stop talking and has already closed my sale, so to speak. I didn't need the rest of the Psalm, or to sing the rest of the song. I only needed those opening words to the Psalm. I lacked nothing. He didn't have to do another thing for me. I could trust Him. My working for free would be fine. It would be okay and I need not fear. My Shephard graces me so that I lack nothing.

That day, He had me. He always has. He always will.

So, I lived under my declaration for a full two years. I'm not saying this to boast, except to boast in the Lord. I'm saying this to show God's faithfulness to those He called. And to show that His power is real, is present, and is sufficient.

One way that God helped me in particular was through a good friend I'll call Rob. Rob heard about our faith journey and became really excited! He said, "Don, I want to help you because I just love what you all are doing."

Rob offered to buy and sell houses in partnership with me. "But I don't have any money to help in this," I said.

"That's okay," he said.

"But I don't have time to help with labor either, or have any skills in that."

"That's okay," he said again.

"So, basically, you are offering to buy, renovate, and to sell houses by yourself, with your own money, with your own labor, split the profits with me, and I do nothing. Is that right?"

And with the biggest grin you've ever seen, he looked at me and said, "Right!" He added, "Don, I just love what you all are doing. I haven't seen faith like this in anyone I have ever know and I want to help."

Amazing friend, more amazing God.

He was a good friend during that time. Years later I lost touch with Rob. He basically just vanished. Over the years, I have often tried to find him to see how he's doing, but he is nowhere to be found. Even Google can't find him. But the Lord knows.

So, again, I don't tell that story lightly because it could sound like a boast about our great faith, but our boast is in God. He is our source.

That's why I said earlier that while hard, the wilderness was also liberating. It was liberating because it taught us to overcome fear. God's faithfulness was a real, tangible, manifested thing. There was no way we could have done this ourselves. When your Daddy is standing in front of you, and behind you, and beside you, and He is the King of the Universe, you overcome fear. That's liberty.

We continued for those two years working hard, begging churches to let us speak in their services, learning how to be more entrepreneurial, learning about grants, and local foundations, and corporate support. And out of necessity, we had become good at them all. Our faith was just as real and just as strong, but we had to do our part in planting and watering the seeds.

One day, at the end of those two years, the Lord told us it was time to stop wandering in the wilderness and to go ahead and cross that Jordan River into the Promised Land.

That was a great day. By then, paychecks were being processed every week. We had sufficient funds to cover our expenses. It took a bit of time before we felt like this new land was our permanent residence, but we did our best efforts to live out the three founding principles we learned on the other side of that river. We remembered the desperation that we felt on the other side, and we knew that we needed to be equally desperate now, even when things were better, because only He made things grow.

CRYING AT THE WINDOW

"Behold, I do a new thing...do you not perceive it?"
Isaiah 43:19

Somebody once said about Homes of Hope, "If there's anything that can be said about your organization, it's that you're not afraid."

That's a great compliment. I believe it was given, not because we have some great inside-track to courage, but simply because we practiced the principles that I've talked about earlier. I believe anyone practicing them can have the same thing said about them.

But a statement like that doesn't account for all the times when we doubted, when we were frustrated or unsure. We had plenty of them. In my opinion, our courage isn't the absence of fear; it is the overcoming of it.

During the wilderness, there was a particular grant that we had applied for which was possibly the most crucial grant in our history, up to that point. It was a very difficult grant to obtain though, not because it was complicated, but because the person controlling the grant was intentionally difficult to work with and quite inconsistent in her thinking, and responses.

I recall that I was also in one of those times when I was struggling with doubt about our true calling again, based on our circumstances. The kind of time I call my "crying at the window" times.

Our office at the time was a former single-wide mobile home that we had gutted and refitted. It had two bedrooms that were converted to offices, as well as a kitchen space. The living room was made into a reception area that was occupied by Cyndi, who functioned as our receptionist, bookkeeper, office manager and momma.

The living rooms and bedrooms provided adequate space for three people, but when we added a fourth person, it was a bit of a challenge. Ted and Gale were asked to share an office. Ted was a hardworking outdoor loving, rough exterior man. Gale, on the other hand, liked to decorate and make the office pretty.

Ted and Gale shared the space for a while, but one day, not too long after this sharing experiment began, Ted said, "Come look at our office!"

I walked in to see duct tape on the floor evenly dividing Ted's space from Gales' space. Ted called Gale's side the pretty side. I'm not sure what Gale called Ted's side. Somehow it worked.

Our fifth person occupied the former kitchen space. It looked more like a walk-in closet we'd stuffed her into. These were the labor pains of our pending relocation to larger facilities. That story will come later.

My office had a side window that overlooked the street. It was my prayer window. I shed a lot of tears standing at that window, staring out. I can remember those times as clearly as I can remember my daughters' names. I had often stood at that window, after everyone else had gone home, and cried while praying over the ministry, and the calling that I knew the Lord had given, but the evidence still wasn't there.

"Now faith is the substance of things hoped for, the evidence of things unseen." **Hebrews 11:1**

Our evidence was definitely unseen. But I exerted my faith at that window countless times, with countless tears. Crying at the window became one of my favorite times because of its sweetness. There is something about exerting faith and crying that the Lord seems to especially be tender towards. In those moments, my frailty of doubt was exposed before Him in the most honest of ways, with my tears. But at the same time, my determination to believe Him was exercised with spiritual adrenaline somewhat like a panicked Dad lifting a crashed car off his son's leg with some super-human strength summoned up purely out of his love. During these times, the Lord seemed to be nearer and more loving than in any other time I can remember. It's as if He said to me, "I know your faith isn't really engaged right now, but I really appreciate your trying."

I know I'm not the only one to have ever felt that.

So, I was crying at the window a lot over this grant. I wasn't one to usually put such high emphasis on a single thing happening, but I couldn't help it this time. I really could not see us surviving financially, if this grant was denied.

Then the person who controlled the grant called and said no. I couldn't believe it. I was stunned. Before that phone call, I had thought for sure that God had heard my desperate prayers for this grant, and would answer. I gathered myself enough to ask her a couple of questions, and suggested some ways she could look differently at our request. She seemed to consider them for a moment, but hung up saying she didn't think so.

I remember not having the strength to rise from my chair to take the four steps over to my crying window. I just cried right where I was.

Ten minutes later, she called back. She had reconsidered and had told me the grant was approved.

I said as little as possible at that point, not wanting to mess things up. Then I thanked her and hung up.

I was so thankful. My fear and doubt turned to dust again. God had provided. Tomorrow someone could compliment us again on our courage, but today was another reminder that doubt isn't the unpardonable sin. God still loved us, and He still provided, even when we were afraid.

Then some humor followed.

I suddenly remembered something I had prayed at the crying window. I'm quite sure this was something the Lord was smiling about as he reminded me of it. I had prayed something like, "Lord, if you will just give us this grant, I'll praise you from the rooftops!"

At that moment, I was compelled. It felt like some magnetic force was pulling me outside. I bolted from my office, and ran past Cyndi shouting, "Praise the Lord!" and burst through the front door onto the porch.

I ran across the porch and down the steps. Ted was pulling up in his car at that exact moment. I ran past his car and scared him out of his skin when I slapped his side window shouting, "Praise the Lord!" I think it's the only time I've ever seen Ted scared, or speechless.

I didn't know what to do, or where to run next, but I kept running! I didn't see anybody to scare on that side of the office, so I ran around back shouting "Praise the Lord" to the neighbors who I am pretty sure weren't home, but I didn't care. I came back on the other side of the office, and there I saw Ted and Cyndi staring at me with mouths agape, looking like they were about to call for help. I shouted, "Praise the Lord!" and they shouted back, "What are you praising Him for?"

I shouted, "Because He deserves it!" This obviously frustrated them, because even though they undoubtedly agreed with me that the Lord deserved praise, they told me later that they thought I'd lost my mind.

Anyway, I didn't know what else to do, and I was getting a bit out of breath, so I jumped on top of my car. Scrambling all the way up onto the roof, I stood tall while shouting "Praise the Lord, Praise the Lord, Praise the Lord!" It was at that point I realized two important things. First, that I needed to get into better shape,- and second, that I had severely dented the roof of my car by standing on it.

After climbing down, and catching my breath, I retold the story to Ted and Cyndi. We celebrated together with hugs and a thanksgiving prayer.

Then Ted calmly said, "Wait right here." He went back into the office, and emerged a minute later with the bathroom plunger and a step ladder. He proceeded to put the ladder beside my car, climb up on it, apply the plunger to the dent in the roof, and pulled out the dent.

All was well. The grant was approved. The dent was out. God was still in charge. Perhaps as you read this story, you thought of your own crying at the window moments.

Please don't lose heart. If God called you, He will provide for you.

He is our loving Father. He knitted us together. He has always been there with us. He has seen every tear, every scraped knee, every disappointment, every minute of anger, and every time we thought nobody cared or we felt all alone. He knows every dream, every longing, and every desire. He knows our past, He knows our future. He knows. He loves us.

Today, in the corner of my office, there is a plunger. Not the original one, because frankly it was serving other purposes for us at the time, but a replacement one to "represent" the story I just told you. People who visit me in my office sometimes glance at it, and I can see from their expressions that I need to tell them the story too.

But even if I'm not retelling it, the plunger remains there, to remind me and those who know the story, of that great day.

That grant indeed made an incredible difference in the life and success of Homes of Hope. To this day, I'm not sure we would have survived financially without it.

REST IN THE MIDST OF THE BUSY-NESS

God's favor equals Spiritual Rest

"Come to me, all you who are weary and burdened, and I will give you rest. Take my yoke upon you and learn from me, for I am gentle and humble in heart, and you will find rest for your souls. For my yoke is easy and my burden is light."

Matthew 11:28-30

The wilderness can be exhausting.

The daily and weekly pressure of not knowing if the bills will get paid, much less the staff getting paychecks, was draining. And the spiritual energy that goes into the desperate wilderness induced prayers is high. Even the weight of serving the people we served and our desire to serve more in the future was heavy. We sometimes even doubted whether we'd get to keep serving them, as there were so many in need.

Rest was something as precious as gold.

One of the best things about God's favor is spiritual rest.

I think spiritual rest is something we all long for, but can't fully believe it can be ours, especially in the midst of our extremely busy lives.

I can't count the number of times I've shared the principle of "rest in the midst of the busy-ness" with people and seen tears well up when they start to understand what it means. I think it might be one of the most transformational principles to experience. We all try so hard to please God when in fact He is pleased with us already.

Think about the story of Christ, when he was baptized by John the Baptist. He had done nothing in His earthly ministry at that point. But as soon as He came up out of the water, the heavens opened up, and His Father spoke for all to hear, *"This is my Son, whom I love, in Him I am well pleased."* Matthew 3:17

God loves us no matter how hard we work. We don't have to do another thing for Him to love us more. Not another thing. Rest in the midst of busy-ness can be enjoyed.

I remember during the wilderness time, I was getting invitations to attend different meetings dealing with community involvement, which were mostly attended by other non-profits. They would meet regularly to discuss the issues of the day, and ways to collaborate with each other to better serve the people and fulfill their respective missions.

I went to a couple of them, but my business background fought against me attending any more. I saw them as a big waste of time. It felt to me at the time, like a bit of a ring-around-the-rosy culture where everyone said the same thing in a big circle and made each other feel better.

Cyndi, who was at the time our receptionist, bookkeeper, office manager, executive assistant, and anything else you could think of that we needed, saw my frustration. She listened to my whining about people continuing to invite me to these types of meetings but she challenged me to go anyway.

She said, "Don, you never know what God is going to do through those meetings. You need to put yourself out there and see what happens."

She made me go. There, I said it. She acted kind of like my momma, which is exactly what I needed. So I went.

And God did stuff. I mean a lot of stuff. In fact, in looking back, more probably came out of those connections and collaborative discussions than any single thing I could point to during our wilderness period.

Thanks Cyndi. For putting me in position to learn a great principle—God's favor equals spiritual rest.

Rest is often misunderstood. We usually think it means doing nothing, like lying on the beach soaking in the sun, listening to the ocean a few feet away. Or maybe reclining in a hammock in the back yard, or taking a nap on the couch. On the contrary, I believe in order to understand God's spiritual rest better; you really need to look at it more as the absence or elimination of something that causes you stress, or that you fear.

We are all busy, and unless that disaster movie about all of the world's power being shut off comes true, I think we will always be busy. So how can you rest in the midst of busy-ness?

By realizing that God's rest takes responsibility away.

Jesus said this in Matthew 11:28-30, (my paraphrase)"If you are weak or tired or burdened, come to me. I will give you rest."

So first we notice that rest belongs to God. It is His to give. Inactivity might look like rest, but that is not God's rest.

Then He said, (my paraphrase) "Put your head into one side of this double-headed yoke. Yes, the one with MY HEAD already in it, and then watch me do the work. Learn from me."

Now we see that God's rest isn't fully realized until we learn from Him. He gives it, yes, but now He shows us what it means.

So what does He show us?

Think of the yoke. A silly looking piece of wood with two holes in it for two heads to go into. Think now of your head and Jesus' head together sticking out of those two holes. Now feel your neck straining as Jesus leads the way to the right or left. Your neck strains because He's pulling you His way, but not telling you which way He's about to turn, He just turns.

You don't have any choice but to go His way, because He's stronger than you, and He knows which way to go. Fighting Him just produces more strain on your neck. In reality, after a bit of fighting, Jesus becomes a real "pain in the neck!"

So, you go His way.

And then He turns again, and the whole thing starts all over again.

Until you go His way again. And again, and again.

But please believe me in this next statement. It is an important part of this principle. What I've just described is not obedience.

If you want to believe it is obedience, you could end up being bound-up in legalistic wrong thinking about who God is, and who you are in Him.

What I've just described, is rest. He is teaching you rest. "Learn from me," He says.

Then He says, (my paraphrase)"I am not mean, I am gentle. This yoke thing doesn't have to be hard, or even feel like work. It's quite easy actually."

Okay, "easy" He says. Go His way and my neck doesn't hurt. I got it. But why doesn't it feel restful?

Listen to Him again and you will find rest.

God's favor equals your rest. When we really get what He is saying, we will find it.

Here's what it is not:

- A ceasing of activity
- A submissiveness found in obedience
- A victory over your enemies
- An absence of enemies

Here's what it is:

- A realization of who is responsible and who isn't

We're not responsible. We never were. Not for the success of His calling. No, that's all His.

He knows which way to turn. And He'll turn the correct way whether we pull against him or not. He's stronger, so it won't matter to Him. And turn He will.

What matters to us, is whether or not the process is tiresome or stressful, and whether or not we're okay with not knowing which way He's going to turn, before He does. Most importantly, is whether we accept the fact that success is never going to be our responsibility. Accept that, and we'll find real rest.

One of my many mottos came out of those meetings that Cyndi made me attend, and out of my learning this principle. I say it often, and it remains true every day; "Stick your head behind every open door, and see if the Lord is in the room. If He is, stick around and see what He's up to. If He is not, get out of there fast."

The responsibility is up to Him. This takes all the pressure off of me (which is usually self-imposed) to know which door to look behind. All I have to remember is the fact that Jesus already said, "My sheep know my voice."

We do know His voice. He opens doors. Look behind them all, and then listen. We already know His voice! If He's there, we'll know it. And He'll do what He intended. If He's not there, we'll know that too and we can leave.

A word of warning to keep in mind is that the devil knows how to open a door too so don't expect them all to be the Lord's door.

We are all busy but we can rest in the busy-ness by going where He leads and not self-imposing the responsibility on ourselves. Jesus said it was His yoke, and his burden, and His work. <u>Putting it on is not adding a burden, it is taking one away</u>.

I truly believe that this was another reason the Lord had us go through the wilderness. It was to share this learned rest with those we serve. When we would meet with the clients we served, the common thread that ran throughout most at their most critical need, was stress and exhaustion.

Now, don't get me wrong, the people we have served over the years are the hardest working people I've known, so I'm not saying they had given up when we met them, I'm saying they were tired.

Finding, and learning about spiritual rest is one of the key ingredients to the message that God wants us to share with them. We could never have shared it if we hadn't lived it.

THE 9/11 LADY

"By this everyone will know that you are my disciples, if you love one another."

John 13:35

Our wilderness experience held many surprises for us at Homes of Hope. Although we didn't always see those surprises as positive back then, I now often say I wouldn't trade that period for anything.

Looking back, it may seem crazy, but it's true.

One of those surprises happened in 2001. At that time, one of the ways Homes of Hope raised funds was by building and installing wrought iron handrails for low-income families. Ted Cochran was our Men's Program Director, and he was also a master welder. Under Ted's tutelage, men in our program were learning a useful trade while producing income for Homes of Hope. We have since discontinued that program.

On September 11, 2001, our men had an assignment to build handrails for Mrs. Dorothy Webster. Mrs. Webster was a widow, quite elderly, and a bit frail. I'm not sure how she heard about our men providing this to the community, but that fateful morning was her scheduled appointment.

Most of us that are old enough to remember that day, and the feelings we had, remember that it was unlike any other morning in our lives.

Those of us not on the jobsite were in the office and were alerted to the news on TV that two airliners had crashed into the twin towers of the World Trade Center in New York City. We'll never forget the feelings we had. None of us will. Watching replays of first hundreds, then thousands of people dying in front of us, will haunt us forever. Fear and uncertainty were the rule of that day.

At Mrs. Webster's house, our men were plugging along doing their work when Mrs. Webster came outside with fear on her face, and a quivering voice, and said, "Please come inside. Something has happened and I'm not sure what."

That day a bond was formed; a bond that would have been unpredictable in anyone's best guess before. That day, our men gathered around Mrs. Webster's TV and watched the horror with her. Tears were jointly shed by an eighty something year old widow and four men, who only a few years before, were addicted to drugs or alcohol, and some with criminal pasts.

That day, our men showed her something she'd possibly never seen in action quite the same. They showed her faith, hope and love, all at once. Our men started to pray; and quickly asked Mrs. Webster if they could pray for her too.

And through it, they simply loved her. Even though they didn't know her, they loved her, and comforted her. It was quite amazing. They were quite amazing.

I wasn't there, so I can only recount this brief summary of what transpired, as it was told to me. But it's something I've always remembered and it affected me to have a point of special reference each year on September 11th. Oh, I'm affected by the remembrance of what happened in New York City that day too. Make no mistake; I'm no different than anyone else. But I also remember Mrs. Webster on that day, and our loving, faith-filled, praying men.

Their lives had been radically changed by Jesus Christ. They were new creations (2 Cor. 5:17) and nothing like the old men they once were. These men were on fire for the Lord daily and couldn't help themselves when ministry opportunities were presented. It was simply who they were now.

2 Cor. 5:17 *"Therefore, if anyone is in Christ, the new creation has come: The old has gone, the new is here!"*

The men and Mrs. Webster actually became great friends that day, and formed a special bond that cannot be explained at all. For almost ten years after that terrible day, our men made a point to block out part of their day each year on September 11th, and go visit Mrs. Webster, and pray with her again.

After that day, Mrs. Webster became one of our first Solid Rock Club members. The Solid Rock Club is made up of monthly donors to Homes of Hope. Some give as little as $10 per month, but all such faithful people are held in high esteem among the staff. They are the ones we can count on every month, no matter what, which is why Mrs. Webster was one of our favorites. Every month we received her personal check in the mail for $10, and of all the checks we received, hers was still my favorite. But believe me, I appreciated each and every one.

Dorothy Webster, or Dot as her friends and family called her, died in April 2014. She will forever be a loved memory and a part of our Homes of Hope story.

THE WILDERNESS GROUP

"How good and pleasant it is when God's people live together in unity."

Psalm 133.1

With every story there are real people who are the living foundation of it. Our wilderness experience has many blessings but none better than the blessing of the bond that was formed between the people who came through it.

Cyndi, Ted, Keith, Nate, Bob, and I are still affectionately called "The Wilderness Group" at Homes of Hope. We are forever knit together.

When we are together, we always fondly recall those days. Something like military camaraderie happens there I guess, I'm not sure, but whatever it is, it never varies. We have a knowing bond with each other that is hard to explain. It's like we were married to each other for twenty years. We finish each other's sentences like old couples. We even know what the others like to order when we eat together.

It's probably quite amusing to the observer, or annoying, or maybe both.

Whenever I ask one of the group what their favorite memory of our wilderness is, it's always the same answer for each one, the closeness.

When the Lord allows you to go through something with others, He does something that often isn't received, and thus missed. His intention seems to be, to literally knit together the hearts of those involved.

Jesus said in Matthew 18: *"Where two or three are gathered, there I am also."* and we all understand that praying together or worshiping together provides some level of spiritual energy, and that He promised to be in our midst. But He also said, *"If two of you on earth agree about anything they ask for, it will be done for them by my Father in heaven,"* and, *"Whatever you bind on earth will be bound in heaven, and whatever you loose on earth will be loosed in heaven."*

What we found went beyond the natural. We found that submitting ourselves to Him in a painful, difficult trial was a growth opportunity individually. Like the organs in a body working together are unified, it was a powerful experience in unity that made us into something beyond a group of stronger individuals. And we discovered a power that fueled our journey that came from this unity.

Cyndi is God's favorite person in the world. I'm convinced of it. He smiles every time He looks at her or thinks about her, which is always, by the way. Cyndi sings like an angel, and is incredibly gifted in song writing. But Cyndi's talent is superseded by her spirit which is so very caring.

Her work at Homes of Hope is so important but her place at Homes of Hope is more important. She was not only the spiritual momma that we men needed during the wilderness, but she was also the spiritual sister we needed to provide a target for us, for brotherly loving teasing! Some of our favorite memories are of times like that.

Cyndi provided fresh and sharp perspective during the wilderness. Sometimes it was powerfully unique, like a home run at a tennis match. Some of her ideas were completely foreign for our thinking, but so innovative and fitting. They would never have seen the light of day if the five men in our group were left to themselves. We really needed her.

Ted was the founder of the idea to add a Men's Development program to our mission, which extended beyond the local Rescue Mission's program for men that was originally utilized for Homes of Hope labor. A product of the Rescue Mission's Overcomers program himself, he had the vision and courage to see that many of the men needed more than 6 months in a recovery program. This program became the pipeline for the men that worked on our homes and allowed the men to "walk this new life out" under a covering of protection and discipleship. His love for the men was stronger than any steel building built to the highest standards. His willingness to help them become victorious over addiction, and the stronghold that it carried, knew no bounds. His unique spirit and personality forever formed the culture of commitment and extreme love that still today permeates our Men's Development program.

Ted had a way of seeing things differently. He saw God's working when others didn't sometimes. He led our men's program to become a Spirit led program that was constantly on the lookout for things unseen and constantly ready to instantly do the unexpected in order to join whatever God was doing. His heart and spirit also led us to make sure that our program was run by men who had overcome addictions themselves. Ted, Bob, Nate, and Keith were all addicted at one time, but all overcame. They were able to see their subsequent work with other men like themselves, as their life-calling. All but Keith became ordained ministers to validate this calling. This amazing dynamic in our program was one of the most important things about it. Ted's handprint will forever be on our ministry.

Keith was our resident guy from up north in this extreme southern culture of South Carolina. Keith was the first man that Ted brought to Homes of Hope's program. A graduate of the Overcomers program too, Keith embraced his northern-ness with gusto and hilarious observations that bordered between courage and crazy. He fit into South Carolina like a cat at a dog show, not better or worse, just different. His love and joy of life were always evident and he was always eager to love someone that was hard to love.

Keith loved to talk too. He was famous for it. We used to have different signals that we flashed to him from the back of the room whenever he spoke in public for Homes of Hope. Each signal varied in method but it was consistent in message to "wrap it up Keith!" Early one Wednesday, he and Ted had to go out on a job. At some point, Keith had crossed some invisible annoyance line with Ted with his constant chatter. Ted looked at Keith and said, "Keith; it's just now 8:30 in the morning and you've already used up all your words for the day!" Keith's quota was evidently different than the rest of us.

Nate is a combination of David and Goliath. He stands about twelve feet tall, or so it seems. A muscular man and a former athlete in his younger days, he once played basketball against Daryl Dawkins, Nate is a physical presence for sure. But his heart is so much bigger than his body,

Nate's story, as dramatic as the others in the details of a life addicted, was a life full of pain and suffering and near-death experiences, but it does not define him. His heart does, and not because it is perfect, or extraordinarily compassionate or anything else like that. His heart defines him because of its love for God. Like David, Nate has a resume of performance and obedience that swings both ways, but more importantly a resume of pursuit. Pursuing God's heart is his joy, his calling, his mission, his constant focus. And this David heart is what draws other men to Nate.

Of all the men who have ever been a part of Homes of Hope, whether coming through our program or becoming staff like Nate did, there has never been a more magnetized person than Nate. He draws people to himself because he possesses something that we all want. We want to love God like He loves us. We see in Nate, that quality, and we want it for ourselves.

Bob is the most unique individual I've ever known. Figuring him out is simply not going to happen. A teacher most assuredly, but also an amazingly gifted craftsman, artist and inventor, there is literally nothing that Bob can't do with his hands and his mind. Bob is also amazingly gifted in what he calls casual discipleship. Working alongside the men all these years, teaching them work skills, work ethic, and life skills, he also makes sure that he's teaching them the word of God constantly and applying it to moment-by-moment life, even while hammering a nail. Bob is the one who had the beginning idea for bringing men from the Rescue Mission out to our facility for job training, and which eventually became the forming of the original vision of Homes of Hope.

Bob also possesses a wonderful attitude and love of God that is so evident, even the hardest hearted person is disarmed by it. I've often said that if you looked up the word joy in the dictionary, you'd see Bob's picture beside it. His life is lived out in gratitude towards the Lord.

Our favorite story of Bob is the day that he smashed his thumb underneath an acetylene tank in the shop. I use the word smashed, but flattened is more accurate. It was bad, and the entire shop came to a screeching halt when it happened. No one could believe how bad his thumb looked and all eyes were on Bob at that instant, prepared for a scream of pain that would curl your toes.

But out of Bob's mouth came, "Well, praise the Lord."

One can only imagine how that can happen. Nobody else in the history of mankind ever said, "praise the Lord" when they smashed their thumb! Nobody.

Ted even went up to Bob and questioned him. I think he must have thought Bob was in shock. He said, "Brother, don't you want to curse, just this one time?"

Everybody cracked up, and Bob went to have his thumb attended to. But we never forgot that.

I think that every church, every ministry, every non-profit, every corporate entity can benefit from the stories of our wilderness, and the people who came through, but not just because they're encouraging. We've all been through tough times and have appreciated the encouragement that came from knowing or hearing about someone who went through something similar.

But I think our story is special because of Matthew 18; "... *where two or three are gathered.*" I've not seen it in anything else before, or since, so I'm guessing it's pretty unique.

WE'RE ALL JUST GUESSING

"Above all, love each other deeply, because love covers over a multitude of sins."

1 Peter 4:8

It is my contention that stupidity isn't really so bad. Either that or I think I may just be too stupid to know.

Over the years at Homes of Hope, we've gained a reputation for excellence, expertise, and leadership because we stress it, and strive for it. We have emphasized good training, learning from our mistakes, and having the courage to try things if we're convinced God is leading us.

But sometimes it felt like we were simply making things up as we go; many times, in fact, especially during the wilderness time.

I don't say this because we were haphazard or unequipped or unplanned or in need of strategy or direction. On the contrary, I believe we are very intentional and strategic and well equipped for the work that God has called us to.

No, I say it because of the Favor principle, and the remembrance that John 15:5 is still true! *"Apart from Me, you can do nothing."*

But this idea of stupidity deserves some explanation.

I'm certainly not advocating a "checking out" of thought, or any effort to achieve understanding. Anyone who knows me knows that's not even close to my thinking.

But I'm struck by the character and nature of God our Father in this thought about stupidity. Scripture says, "Love covers over a multitude of sins." My observance is that it also covers our own stupidity.

Isaiah 55:8-9 says. *"For my thoughts are not your thoughts, neither are your ways my ways, declares the Lord. As the heavens are higher than the earth, so are my ways higher than your ways and my thoughts than your thoughts."*

What I'm saying is that we often get frozen in our thoughts, and thus our tracks, by trying too hard to figure it out. We study scripture, we pray, we meditate, and sometimes we still end up just guessing if we were honest in our evaluation of ourselves.

Again, like the time when the Lord said, "Will you stop trying to make me fit on a spreadsheet?" Here I was trying to follow His lead, but I filtered His lead through my human effort machine and missed the point entirely. He was leading me toward Himself and His sovereignty over our ministry and to the point of listening moment by moment, day by day, without the benefit of a fixed roadmap.

Galatians 5:18 says, *"But if you are led by the Spirit, you are not under the law."*

That means that if you do everything He says to do, you will never make a mistake, and you'll not be held accountable. Because it will be God doing it, not you.

But the converse of the scripture is also true. Whatever you do on your own, is therefore held accountable.

Well, I don't know about you, but I like the idea of never messing up again. All I have to do is follow His lead. The problem is, He will not always lead by roadmap. And He refuses to fit on a spreadsheet. He wants us to listen, moment by moment day by day and do what He says.

So what does this have to do with stupidity?

I am convinced that if I am trying my hardest to listen, not to figure it out on my own, but to listen and follow what I feel that I heard, after patient contemplation and prayer, He will always cover over my mistakes.

Because in Galatians 5:18, being led by the Spirit doesn't mean I have to hear it correctly 100% of the time. It means I have to listen carefully and faithfully, and obey what I hear. If I hear it wrong, or interpret it wrong, His heart will overcome my actions and He will cover them.

This changed my life.

The greatest pressure we feel as children of our Holy God, our Father, the King of the Universe, the Great I Am, is getting it right. And, it is the single least important thing He requires. Why? Because it is the one thing we can never do. As Max Lucado wrote: "We are human beings, not human doings."

Both Old and New Testament scripture, points to the one answer, the one person, Jesus Christ, as the eternal answer to this dilemma. Only Jesus gets it right every time. In Him, we get it right.

We shouldn't stop building strategy or thinking about the future, or planning. But we should stop trying to figure it out when we don't have to. Be led by His Spirit, and we'll never fail.

THE FAMILY PRINCIPLE

"Love never fails......for God is love."
1 Cor. 13:8; 1 John 4:8

After we started to grow, and about the time we were moving to the next level of working in the promised land, we added two more core value principles at Homes of Hope. The first three you've read about previously.

The fourth principle is family and the fifth principle is fun (not having fun is a fire-able offense at Homes of Hope). We insist everyone has fun. Eating lunch together every Friday as a staff is an example of putting these two 'F' principles together. We love each other and we have a lot of fun. Friday lunches are the highlight of the workweek.

Also important is making a concerted effort to bring in all new employees to our story and faith journey experiences. We want them to feel as if they were there with us in the beginning; that they are part of the story automatically. One way we do that is during on-boarding of new employees, on either their second or third day on the job. We sit down and tell them the story, and explain our five 'Fs' and make sure they know that we are all a part, not just the old-timers.

The family principle is basically this; *if we minister well to the whole community, but fail to minister to each other* (our staff, our board, our volunteers, our supporters), *we've failed in our mission.*

This simple principle is more than just being good to each other, and making sure we don't lose sight of that while pouring ourselves out to the community. Its huge importance is the accurate representation of the Father's love, and the freedom that brings.

This starts in our own Homes of Hope family. Communicating this to our staff looks different to them than what they've experienced in other jobs. Like any other employer, we expect excellence in job performance, but we make every effort to value our employees for who they are, not what they do. It is the single most accurate way to represent the Father's love. And, if we effectively do that, they in turn can enjoy great freedom, and also accurately represent it to those we serve.

A number of times over the years I've seen weight lifted off of staff member's shoulders when they grasped this family principle, and in turn, this same lifting of weight off client's shoulders when that same staff person communicates this effectively with them. It's really quite a remarkable thing to witness and one never lacking in emotion.

An example of this was a conversation I had with Michael (not his real name). Michael had joined our staff with a new idea that we tried but eventually shut down. It was well worth the try, but in the end, it didn't fit. I remember asking Michael to come into my office and we talked about why this idea wasn't going to work out.

During the process of this, Michael shared with me how hard he had always tried to be successful. He shared how his Dad had always viewed him and how he never seemed to measure up. He spoke about his college roommate who was wildly successful. Michael felt that he was just as smart, energetic, ambitious and resourceful, but that his ventures never seemed to work out.

At some point, I shared with him my own experience as a dad, and how understanding God's parenting of His children helped me to understand how to parent my own children. Ultimately, it liberated me from my own insecurities, over my failures, and my efforts to be good enough.

I shared with him the importance of knowing God's character and nature, over trying to understand His ways. I said, "Michael, you don't have to do a single thing from today forward, to get God to love you more than He already does. Not one thing. He loves your heart, not your work. You can't mess up enough to cause Him to stop loving you."

This broke him suddenly. The tears flowed. That conversation eventually led to Michael making a fresh, new commitment to God and how he would view Him from now on. A yoke of oppression was broken that day. *"It is for freedom, that Christ has set us free."* (Galatians 5:1)

Hopefully, we also practice this principle with board members, volunteers and supporters. Over the years, we've received multiple comments something like "there's just something different about your organization, I can't put my finger on it, but it feels different when I'm around all of you." This is one of our favorite compliments because it tells us that we're accomplishing the fourth principle.

Once, during a conversation with a good friend, I made what I thought was an unremarkable statement. I said, "Of all things in life, there is really only one that I'm absolutely sure of and that is that God loves me."

I respected my friend greatly and believe him to be one of the most spiritual people I've ever known, but he surprised me with his questioning my statement.

He asked, "You're absolutely sure of it?"

"100% absolutely sure," I replied.

He seemed shocked. As a result, so was I. I thought my absolute surety was a fairly common thing among followers of Christ, but I soon found out that it might not be that common at all. He had traveled the world many times over and talked with thousands more people than I'd ever hoped to. It was his opinion that most people doubted this foundational truth, whether partially or on occasion.

Well, I'm nothing special, I can assure you, quite the opposite actually. Maybe I'm just too stupid to think more deeply on these matters, but it has never entered my mind that God may not love me. Even from a young age, before I even knew the gospel story of why Jesus came and died, I knew God loved me. And somehow, that I loved Him too.

I remember when my two daughters were young; they liked to try to get me to say which one I loved more. I always answered them the same way, "You're both tied for first."

It is the way I feel loved by God. He loves me so much that I'm first on His list. You, and everyone else in the world, all that lived before us, and all that will come after us, we're all tied for first.

Below, I believe are the reasons God has us all tied for first. Ultimately, His love, when understood and enjoyed, brings two things:

- Freedom from the bondage of performance based love. In my opinion, this is the greatest bondage among believers today. God loves us, period. We are to show that same love to others, period.

- A foundation that can be stood on, that will never falter. The structure of our lives will encounter storms, weathering and deterioration, like any structure, but the foundation of His love will never fail or crack or sink.

If this is not true, nothing is true and we cannot count on anything. But if this truth is really believed 100% absolutely, it will change and liberate your life to a point of the greatest joy and peace ever imagined on this earth.

John 3:16: *"For God so loved the world that He gave His only begotten Son."*

CROSSING THE JORDAN

VISIBILITY LEADS TO CREDIBILITY

"He who works his land will have abundant food, but he who chases fantasies lacks judgment."

Proverbs 12:11

It was clear in the early days that the Lord had given us a model to build that was based on being an entrepreneurial non-profit. This meant to us that we were to produce the majority of the income necessary for operations ourselves.

This word from the Lord we interpreted as "work the land."

In short, we referred back to the story in the Old Testament when the Israelites crossed the Jordon River out of the wilderness. Although they were used to manna falling from the sky each day in the desert, when they reached their promised land, the manna stopped falling. In a real sense, the Lord was telling them, "Work the land I've given you for it is fertile."

We sensed this same word as we left our wilderness, and our land was in the form of our ministry and housing. We knew we could produce income with it.

But this was only part of what "work the land" meant. There was another part. The part we welcomed was the housing part, because we knew how to work, and we knew how to work hard.

The part that was particularly frustrating was the non-profit part. This meant that to be a true non-profit, and to offer the community the benefit of tax deductions for their support, we had to rely on the community for a portion of our income too.

Business we knew but fundraising we didn't.

But the Lord was clear, and so was the Internal Revenue Service. Financial support from the community was one of the clear identifying marks of a non-profit. For this part, the Lord told us just this one thing which was, "do not neglect to include His people in His ministry."

We thought that this must mean His church. So we spoke in churches almost every week. Some of those services, all of which included testimonies from the men in our program for overcoming addictions, were the best services we'd ever been a part of. The Spirit's moving was clear and real, and people's lives were genuinely touched by God's life changing transforming power! We were sure that this was what the Lord had instructed us to do.

But something unexpected happened. Financial support did not follow.

Now, to be clear, we did indeed make some life-long friends and some of them became life-long supporters. Let there be no mistake about how blessed we were, and still are, to have found these precious parts of our Homes of Hope family. They remain some of our most cherished supporters, for they not only give, they also pray. This group has been faithful and without them, I'm convinced we would have failed.

But the financial support that we needed to fulfill the portion of income we couldn't generate ourselves fell far short through these efforts.

We were a bit perplexed. Again, the Lord was clear. So what were we missing?

I think that so many of us make this same ongoing mistake that I've mentioned it a couple of times already, which is to try to make God's plan fit on a spreadsheet. He refuses to fit on one.

We took His instructions to be the final answer for the result we needed, and failed to consider that there was more to it.

When asking God for direction, one should be careful not to mistake recognizing His first step and thinking it is His final plan. God had given us a directive that was simply a first-step. He said never fail to include His people. But He never said that this would solve our entire problem.

What He had given us, was the foundation. Just as He did in several instances before, He gave us the thing we could build on but He did not reveal the entire set of blue prints to us.

In construction, there is something called Design-Build, which means that instead of simply having a full set of plans at the beginning of the work, you have a set of plans that takes you to a point. At that point, the architect designs the next portion based on the results of the previous building efforts.

I think that the Lord likes the Design-Build model a lot.

So, we were left with a lot of great church services behind us, but what were we still missing?

What we found out was a great surprise to us. As we began to reach out more to the community, we included asking the media for help in telling our story, and stories of the families and/or the men we helped. And, we learned something about human nature in the process.

The media was indeed eager to tell the stories and we were excited about the plethora of articles being produced from a wide range of publications. The TV media was enthusiastic too, and we became quite comfortable being on camera which was something none of us could have predicted.

In fact, we were becoming quite the popular source for stories and began to get calls from the media for more, even when little had transpired since the last story. We thought this could be what we needed.

Exposure might bring us support!

So we thought we were ready to capitalize on this exposure at another level. We sent out a blind mass-mailing. To this day, it was one our biggest failures that we have ever attempted.

We bought a mailing list, a bulk-mailing permit and contracted with someone to produce the slickest looking newsletter with a direct ask for funds on the back. We produced 20,000 of them. We even took a whole day off to form a mass assembly-line for folding, stuffing, stamping and mailing them. A great team-building activity.

We sent out all 20,000. We received one check in response, for fifty dollars.

Even today whenever I think about it, I can't decide if I should beat my head against the wall a bit, or just laugh. Most of the time, I laugh.

We thought that being in the media would have given us name recognition. Since our stories were so welcomed and uplifting, we assumed more of those stories would inspire those receiving the newsletter to give. Especially since we asked them to.

One check for fifty dollars. Yes, I still laugh. Beating your head against the wall only results in a bloody head.

Over time, the Lord taught us a practical lesson from this about people, yes even His people. Visibility leads to credibility.

We thought our success was enough. But it wasn't. For most folks, success isn't fully proven by having a good story in the paper. For most, it takes stability too. And for a non-profit to have a great story in the paper, it usually only meant it was mostly forgotten by people the minute they laid their eyes on the next story on the next page.

Folks needed to see a building, with a parking lot, and offices inside. With people going in and out of the building, and people sitting in the offices working. We were successful, as measured by the achievement of our mission. But when measured by most other people, we fell short. They couldn't "see" our work as our location at that time was very much off the beaten path. We knew that until we had this visibility piece of the puzzle, the portion of income we needed from the community would fall short too.

We also felt led to start building new housing. Mobile homes were a great answer for families who could only afford $100 per month, but so many larger families needed affordable housing too, or needed to live in the city where they worked, and most needed other services beyond housing.

We learned even later that God had ultimately called us to an Isaiah 61 style of transformation of communities, cities, and counties. And that His calling would one day include state-wide influence regarding housing issues and systems.

But for now, we simply learned that we were to build traditional homes, and not just rehab mobile homes. And that these new homes would produce income for Homes of Hope but more to come on that.

First, the Lord had to give us His next set of Design-Build plans that would affect both parts of His "work the land." He wanted to give us His visibility, which leads to the credibility part of the plan.

Move to Greenville.

THE MOVE TO GREENVILLE

".... I press on toward the goal for the prize of the upward call of God in Christ Jesus."

Phil. 3:14

Being a success on a back lot in Powdersville, South Carolina was invisible to a lot of people.

For the first seven years of our existence, our office and rehab facility were on the back lot of the business owned by our founder, Tim Revis. We had a great deal which was-one dollar a year in rent. After roughly our first two years, Tim had to sell his business, which of course started our wilderness journey, but the new business owner graciously honored the terms for leasing the back lot that Tim had previously set for us. But who doesn't know though, that some great deals are only great for a season?

It was time for us to find out what we would be when we grew up.

As explained in the previous chapter, we were learning how to "work the land" and for both parts, the entrepreneurial part and the public support part, gaining credibility through visibility was crucial.

When I first told our staff of the dream to relocate to Greenville, I told them that after we moved, we would be amazed at the number of volunteers we'd have, the amount of support we'd gain, and the volume of new resources we'd have access to. I told them they'd notice this within 2 years.

Boy was I wrong!

It was six months and not two years. It happened with lightning speed. Part of the reason for that was the part that we already had in place, the actual success in our mission. That success, which was not enough before, now had this crucial visibility piece added, and almost instantly we saw all the things happen that I had predicted.

Support increased dramatically, volunteers started asking about ways to serve, and people started instantly taking us more seriously than ever before.

To get to that point though, we had to take another large leap of fearless faith.

We needed to trust God that He would provide the cost of acquiring land, building a facility and the ongoing monthly mortgage payment.

Now, some of you might stop at this point and think, *Why not raise the funds instead of borrow them?*

Many ministries, churches and non-profits do just that, and do it successfully.

"After all," you might say, "you're talking about trusting God, right? Can't He provide the funds? Do you lack in your trust so much that you assume you have to borrow the money without even trying to raise the funds?"

Our move to Greenville, and the details of it, is an example that I believe separates our story from the norm and makes it worth considering as a different model for ministries to consider. Working the land is a principle that many might reject for this very reason. They might see it as a dependency on self, and work, and leave God out.

If you're thinking this way, I hope you will remember The Favor Principle chapter. It is the most important principle in our story and demands this reminder here, because if this principle is rejected or discounted, this part of our story, and frankly most of our story, will not be of any benefit.

For us, we were told to "work the land", build housing, and produce income from it. God wasn't telling us He was short on cash at the moment. He was teaching us this principle on a higher level. He was teaching us that our planting and watering would be made to grow by Him.

God said He would pay for our move, but not until we moved. So, borrow the money we did, bought the land, and built the building. We kept working the land, and God kept making it grow (income), and He paid the bills each month. Our move to Greenville was the launching pad for another level of faith, and subsequent tremendous growth that still continues to this day.

By the way, a shout out to a now retired banker, Frank Wingate, who was with the former New Commerce Bank, for taking a huge chance on us in making the loan. It enabled us to buy the land and build the offices that are still our headquarters today. I will forever be grateful to Frank for showing faith in us. And we didn't let him down.

On a separate note, I'd like to include the story of how we found the right place to relocate to. Within the story, is another lesson we learned.

I had cast the vision for the move with staff, and also with our Board of Directors. One board member, Charlie Warth was also a great friend. Charlie died in 2013 after a battle with cancer. He was a great man.

I had asked the board to keep their eyes open for a good spot near, or in Greenville. Soon after that, I found a spot of land myself. It was really an ugly piece of land, but it was in a highly visible area, one that would be seen by several thousand people passing by in daily commute traffic.

A local bank had foreclosed on it and it was up for sale. I inquired about it and was told the asking price was $300,000. I thought it a little high, but proceeded to run the numbers because I thought this might be the perfect location for us.

Charlie, unbeknownst to me, was also eyeing a parcel for sale. He was convinced that Homes of Hope should be closer to the city, where most of the families we served lived. My piece of land was close, but not accessible for public transportation, an element that was, and still is, crucial to those we serve. Charlie called me to say he also had found a parcel of land and wanted me to look at it.

Have you ever had a time in your life when good news wasn't welcomed? This was one of those phone calls. I didn't want his piece of land. I wanted the one I'd found. It reminded me of times in my childhood when I'd found the perfect toy, or liked the perfect girl, only to have someone tell me something bad about either that I didn't want to hear.

But I respected Charlie and he was my good friend. So, I went to meet him at his land.

It was uglier than mine! I was relieved. It was smaller, and more sloped, and had a creek running through it. Yes, it was only $75,000, but it was easy to see why it could never work, I thought to myself.

Someone asked me the other day how I heard the voice of the Lord. One of my answers to him was when a thought jumps into my head that is completely foreign to anything I was thinking or wanted to think, but it comes with overwhelming peace and a sense of love.

This was one of those times. The Lord spoke to me through Charlie that day as I listened to him explain why his land was perfect for us, and mine wasn't. There was no doubt by the end of our conversation that this was the site we were to move to. Ugly, watery and sloped thought it was, it was our new home. We both knew it.

So we bought the land, and built the offices.

The lesson here is when the Lord is directing you to something or someplace, it is never for you. It is for those He called you to serve.

We are still on that site today. We've expanded the building three times and plan on being there for the long-term. It is as perfect a site as anyone could ever have dreamed. And, it's not too ugly anymore. At least, not to me.

Moving to Greenville was a key piece of our journey. And trusting God for provision in a different way than the norm was a key piece too. It was a catalyst to understanding what working the land really meant.

PART II

OPERATING FROM CALLING

PART II is meant to show how we applied these principles at Homes of Hope.

It is not meant be a guide for how things should be applied for anyone reading this with thoughts of starting a ministry, or is already in ministry. This is not the Lord's will for this, we believe. In following His leading and learning His principles for calling, our journey manifested in just the way He intended it for us. Your journey will likely manifest differently. Allow Him to be your guide, using our story as an example, and nothing more.

THE PROMISED LAND

DON'T BE AFRAID

"Fear not, little flock; for it is your Father's good pleasure to give you the kingdom."

Luke 12:32 (King James Version/KJV)

Christ said it eloquently; "Fear not." Me, I just say it like I hear it: "Don't be afraid."

After the lessons of our wilderness journey, we were hopeful that the instruction manual would be passed out among us, and we would be instructed to turn to page one, with the first sentence underlined.

That didn't happen.

A casual observer would have said we took our first steps with great confidence, but that was only our disguise. Our first steps were taken with great courage, but not a lot of confidence. The difference was who we were relying on.

When you rely solely on God, you are not afraid. When you rely on yourself, you usually have confidence at first, but that wanes quickly when you prove yourself to be less than adequate as a source.

I've often told people that I wouldn't trade our wilderness experience for anything. The main reason I say that is because of it, I could honestly say I wasn't afraid of anything anymore, and was pretty sure I never would be.

Well, you can imagine that most of the times when I said that, I got a funny look, courteous, but still funny. I don't think anybody ever believed me when I said it. They still don't in fact.

I know in comparison to soldiers facing bullets in wartime, police officers staring down the barrel of a pistol, firemen trapped in a house fire, that my statement seems shallow and self-serving. I don't want to be disrespectful here; I'm only saying what I feel.

Hopefully I can explain. It's not the depth of the danger faced that produces courage to this degree. It's the depth of the trust. Once you have seen that God can be trusted in all situations, no matter what, you are never afraid. And the "no matter what" part is the key. To choose faith with a reckless abandon is like jumping off a cliff, but it is really the only way to trust Him to the degree that you can make a no fear declaration.

Paul said, "To live is Christ, to die is gain." We have the best of both worlds as Christians. We live with Christ here and fear not because if we die, which is the worst thing most of us can think of, we live with Him there.

Operating from calling is Part II of our story. Don't be afraid is the beginning, the foundation. Everything that follows must be built on this foundation.

If you examine the verse under the title to this chapter, you will see a key point; that the Father wants to give us the Kingdom. Not begrudgingly, but because it is His good pleasure.

Now, I love the story of Peter in the boat with the other disciples. I alluded to it in Part I. Peter was called when Jesus said, "Come." And Peter came, and walked fearlessly on water.

And the importance of the story isn't walking on water. The importance is two-fold.

- He was called.

- Christ rescued him when he sank.

Remember, Part I is for the principle teachings the Lord gave us in this.

Part II is for operating out of the principles, and the calling. So, for that, we will focus on the Father, and that He takes good pleasure in giving us His Kingdom.

As I mentioned, operating without fear comes from trust, and trust comes not from circumstances, or even God's actions towards us. It comes from His character and nature. Trusting Him for who He is, and not how He is, is all-important. It is the liberating thing that moves us from faith that believes He can, to trust that believes that He will.

The things He led us to do after our wilderness experience were tests of this foundation, to see if it was sturdy enough to hold up. He wanted to build much on it, but it had to be proven first. And the tests were simply, "Do you trust me, based on who I am?"

I remember being led to explore our mission and find ways to produce more income from it. Part of that was my business background urging me to do it ourselves because we seemed more likely to succeed at that, than fundraising which seemed very scary.

As I said before, we knew how to do business but we didn't know how to raise money.

I remember making a phone call to the State Housing Finance and Development Authority, to see if there was help for our mission. For those who have worked with government entities, you know that cold-calling them and asking for help for an idea that was a bit outside the box, was pretty frightening by itself. Adding to that, the idea that we were working with two things others usually didn't want to be associated with (mobile homes and formerly homeless and addicted men) made the phone call even scarier.

But we felt led to call. And trust.

The receptionist took my call, and after listening to me for a minute, said, "I know just the person to direct you to."

It was Valerie Williams. I'll never forget that call. Valerie listened to me, and asked good questions, and took the time to be genuinely interested. She told me exactly what to do, who to talk to, and what order to do each. Valerie was a program coordinator at the time. She likely went above and beyond her normal scope during that phone call. Many years later, Valerie became the head of the whole agency. I'll always be grateful to her for her customer service that day.

The Lord was in that phone call. I know there are those of you who don't believe God bothers Himself with mundane details, but when He calls you, He is in every detail. We'll talk more about that idea later.

Anyway, I did what Valerie recommended, down to the letter, and it worked beautifully. After following her suggestions, and submitting the application for funding, we received a $90,000 grant to help us continue doing what we were called to do.

Today, $90,000 is a drop in the bucket of our total annual budget. But that day, out of the wilderness, out of our desperation, and out of our uncertainty, it was like a billion dollars to us!

We couldn't believe it. We thought we'd died and gone to heaven, so to speak. It was one of the early signs from our Father, that it was His good pleasure to give us the Kingdom. In this, we felt

Him telling us, "The foundation is laid so keep building on it." We did what He said.

In multiple ways we started to make bold moves. Not reckless, but bold. Like the faith He taught us in the beginning, like "bus station faith," we continued to step out of the boat and expected to either walk on water or be rescued; either way was fine with us.

We started attending meetings in the community and learning about other ways the Lord was working among His people. We also learned from folks who clearly were not identifying themselves as His people. We were His sheep though and we knew His voice.

We began to learn about building homes with new construction, in addition to rehabbing mobile homes. We began to learn about other resources that would allow us to produce and earn income from housing that would in turn finance the mission. We began to refine the work that the men in our program produced, and found ways to generate support for that, while still accomplishing the mission.

You might remember that I said one of my favorite mottos grew out of this season. "Stick you head behind every open door, and see if the Lord is in the room. If He is, stick around and see what He's up to. If He's not, get out of there fast!"

This motto summed up several of our founding principles into one philosophy.

Basically, it expressed that the Lord was in charge, and that we weren't. All we had to do was to know His voice (and scripture already tells us that we do) and listen for it, and obey it.

We found that we didn't always need to analyze too much. We needed to get moving. Someone once said, "It's hard to steer a ship in dry-dock."

I'm not advocating for recklessness. I'm advocating for dependency. Ministries, churches, non-profits and individuals of calling, often make the same mistakes. We try so hard to figure it out and even base our research, our analysis, and our findings on scripture. Rightly so as scripture is given to us for direction, but we fail to do the one thing God would rather us do more than any of these other things.

Trust Him. Really trust Him. Get out of the boat, get in the bus station line, and trust Him. Do not be afraid.

When your earthly father is walking beside you, but his character is questionable, there is still fear that he may not protect you, or provide for you every time. That he might let you down. You don't question his love (even though some of you may have had earthly fathers that merited doubt), but you might be a little shaky on his provision, or protection.

When your heavenly Father is with you, and especially when He called you, you can trust His character. He will never fail to be who He is. So, even if that $90,000 grant had not come, He would have provided some other way.

Your circumstances and His actions are not the determining factor in "fear not" living because His character and nature are.

If you are called, don't be afraid.

As I said in Part I, people saying that they notice our lack of fear in doing the work, might be the best compliment we've ever received.

Don't start building your ministry, your church, your non-profit organization, or your individual calling and purpose, on any other foundation. If you operate out of fear, you will be doing the one thing that grieves the heart of God more than any other. He is a good Daddy. And when His child walks beside Him and fears, it grieves His heart. Do not be afraid.

EMBRACING THE FAITH ADVENTURE

"...because you know that the testing of your faith produces perseverance."

James 1:3

LIVING ON THE EDGE OF UNCERTAINTY

I've been convinced for a while now that the main reason the Lord allowed us to go through our wilderness time was to be able to uniquely relate to those we served, and be able to testify that faith got us through.

Many of the folks we serve indeed have their own faith adventure, and many are more miraculous than our story. But sometimes we find a person who can only relate to the wilderness part.

Usually, it's not a hard sell to convince a person in the wilderness that faith can help them when you have your own true story.

There is something in the affordable housing industry called NIM-BY. It stands for Not in My Backyard. Obviously, it means that sometimes there is resistance to affordable housing being built in areas of affluence, or for other reasons.

But I've also observed a fascinating thing about faith. That it resides where it is embraced. In other words, there seems to be a spiritual NIMBY present when things are going well, or when we're preoccupied, or sometimes other reasons.

The theme of this book is that we must be even more desperate in the promised land than we were in the wilderness, and that faith is the vehicle that our desperation jumps into. But the biggest obstacle to that is prosperity. Second to prosperity is preoccupation.

Many talk of their faith journey but I think I now prefer faith adventure. A journey sounds maybe a bit too uneventful to me. When I take a trip, I know where I'm going and the process between point A and point B is my journey. Not much adventure there.

But an adventure. Now there is some uncertainty. In an adventure, there are pitfalls and roadblocks around every corner. But there are also waterfalls, horizons, and sunsets. An adventure is the stuff of living. And a faith adventure? Even better!

I think that maybe the Lord had us go through the wilderness for another reason; to learn how to embrace the adventure. How to live on the edge of uncertainty. How to take risks and be fearless based on His leading. Not recklessness but exuberance.

This came easy in the wilderness when we had nothing to lose. But even in the early years of the promised land, it was already a way of life for us because we were still learning how to operate with excellence, in faith.

As Homes of Hope has grown over the years however, this became harder to do. Prosperity demanded more accountability, more structure, and more thoughtfulness. Much was required to whom much was given.

A great struggle continues as we learn this balance between years of experience and childlike faith. The kind that jumps into the faith vehicle not knowing where it's going. Our years of experience sometimes translates into cruise control. Our prosperity and preoccupation sometimes causes us to operate on auto-pilot where we go through the motions of success and feel just fine in doing so.

Both faith and experience are real, both are valid. It's not fifty-fifty, but rather each 100%. But the faith adventure doesn't come as naturally anymore. It is something we have to intentionally do now. It is something we have to continually talk about and acknowledge. It is something we have to work at.

PRAYER

One of the ways that we work at is prayer. We constantly make prayer a part of our daily functions. We continue to remind each other when something good happens that it is because the Lord has answered prayer. We continue to encourage each other to pray over decisions and initiatives before engaging them. And we certainly continue to look for opportunities to pray for and with those we serve.

Personally, I have always prayed "my list."

I learned about list praying from Reverend Jarrard. I have no recollection of his first name, unless it was Brother because that's all I ever heard him called besides Reverend.

Reverend Jarrard was a man I knew many years ago who was in his late eighties. He was known for his childlike faith, and for being a prayer warrior. I also knew him for his great generosity, though he did this in secret so he wasn't widely known for that.

I heard that he had a list that he prayed through every day. When I first heard this, I didn't like it. I thought it too liturgical or legalistic. I thought prayer was supposed to be a conversation with God and not a reading. Of course, I was right about that, but I was short-sighted in my rightness.

Embracing the Faith Adventure 95

I was able to see Reverend Jarrard's list after his death. I was stunned. It was so much longer than I'd imagined. I couldn't believe it. My pastor at the time showed it to me and told me that he knew this list praying took Reverend Jarrard over an hour each day to pray through, sometimes two.

But something else stunned me even more.

On his list were the simplest things. Things that happened daily. Oh, he had some people on there that needed great healings and some missionaries overseas that he wanted to lift up, but the simple things amazed me. And haunted me at the same time.

Why would this man pray daily for over an hour, over some of the simplest things in his life, like things that you could do on cruise control, or auto-pilot?

Years later, as I felt the tremendous weight of leading Homes of Hope, beginning in the wilderness and continuing right up to this day, I remembered this list of Rev. Jarrard's. And I suddenly realized that this was not liturgical or legalistic at all!

I realized that this simple thing, list praying, was a sign of Reverend Jarrard's desperation. Desperation for the Lord to guide him in every way, especially in the simple things. But more importantly, in praying daily for help for even the smallest thing, Reverend Jarrard was acknowledging that he needed God to do everything! Not as a lazy man asking someone to do something he could do himself, but as a desperate man asking the one and only person (God) who could truly do these things.

This changed my life dramatically. This became for me one of the primary faith vehicles I still use today, to be on my faith adventure.

Recently, our Director for Men's Workforce Development, Steve Vicari, told me of a dramatic image the Lord had given him suddenly and unexpectedly. A picture of the Lord leaning in to my list prayer time with focused attention to every detail. He said it made him weep. The thought of this makes me emotional too as I think about this real image being an actual reality.

To this day, I still pray every day over every client, every future client, every past client, every department, every employee, every board member, every advisory council member, every program, all of the finances and every aspect of the finances (budgets, income, expenses, cash-flow, reserves, fundraising requests), every development project, every planned development project, every appointment of the day, staff leadership, staff leadership learning, discernment, future staff, future board members and mission/vision success.

Now you know my list. Certainly, there are more personal things I also pray each day and there is focused time asking for forgiveness for my failures, expressing gratitude and praise, and simply having that conversation that He longs for His children to have. But my list is that faith adventure vehicle that brings it back home to me each day exactly how desperate I am, and subsequently we at Homes of Hope are, for Him to do what only He can do.

Within each list item, I usually ask Him for favor and anointing. The Favor Principle was already discussed in Part I, but the anointing is something that I ask for that reminds me of His supernatural touch on all these things. And I daily quote John 15:5 during my list praying, "Apart from (You), (we) can do nothing."

WEDNESDAY MORNINGS

Another faith adventure vehicle is Wednesday morning.

I started this discipline during the wilderness too, and I continue to this day. I have a permanent booking on my calendar that I share on the company calendar as well. Each Wednesday morning, I block out two hours for time alone with the Lord. Time for me to listen, and then converse, and then to ask for the courage to do what I heard Him say.

During this time, I always start out with the same opening line; "Lord, you're the CEO of Homes of Hope, not me. But I have the title, and I don't know what to do. But you do. Please tell me what to do, and then give me the clarity to hear you, and the courage to do what you say." This also changed my life.

There is great power in daily prayer and prayer without ceasing (as Paul wrote). In my opinion, a person cannot live an effective Kingdom life as one could without both, but this time alone for me, was and is also powerful.

During this time, I sometimes write down what I hear. I sometimes just listen. Sometimes I open the Bible. Sometimes I sit there. Sometimes my mind wanders and I waste the time. It is not a success formula. It is simply my attempt to focus in quietness and I often hear things I didn't before.

Now, make no doubt, on occasions when I didn't hear Him before, that He was speaking clearly, I was just not listening. My Wednesday morning appointments with the Lord make it easier to listen and focus. That's all. It is not a magic bullet, actually it's just my way to overcome my frailty.

I often just ask Him basic questions like, "Is there anywhere we should turn left or right, go back or ahead? Is there anything we're doing we should stop doing, or is there anything we're not doing we should start doing?"

The most important thing I ask Him though, is this; "Lord, please give me the courage to do what I hear you say." So many times, in my opinion, this is the real problem in our listening to the Lord. We don't like what He's telling us. Having the courage to do it even when we don't like it, is hard, but it's key.

These basic questions are a breeding ground for my spirit and mind to tune in and hear specific things that I just wasn't hearing before. They begin the process of conversation with the King of the Universe. And I promise you, you have the same access to Him as I do, and He will speak the truth to you every time. Just ask, and listen. It's not that difficult.

John 16:13: *"He will guide you into all truth."*

Faith line

The last faith adventure vehicle I'll talk about is our company "faith line." A critical piece to our success.

We call ourselves an entrepreneurial non-profit because we produce enough income from our housing to cover about 70% of our budgeted operating costs. While this is a great benefit and one that has allowed us to grow at a more rapid pace than a lot of other non-profits, my favorite part of this is the 30% that we must depend on the community for.

Non-profits depend on the community for income all the time, but most of them depend on the community for 100% of their needed income. Our 30% model sends a clear message to donors, that we are earning all that we can in order to lessen our dependence on them.

The 30% if my favorite part for two reasons.

First, because depending on the community for 30% allows them to be involved. God instructed us right from the start, to never neglect including His people in the work of His kingdom. And this 30% need, allows His people to participate.

And we really need it. After all, have you ever tried to pay 100% of your bills with 70% of the money?

Secondly, because we always include a "faith line" in our budget that is part of this 30%. By that I mean that we budget expected income from things we can historically measure. For example, the Annual Golf Tournament, the Annual Gala, grant writing, annual campaigns, and more, but these things will never equal the entire 30% income needed. Our "faith line" becomes the part of the 30% income that we have no idea where it will come from. This thrills me.

This "faith line" demands that we must continue to activate our faith, trust God, ask Him for help, and depend on Him.

Of course, we depend on Him for 100% of it all. We all know that. But this faith line is something that we write down on paper for all to see, and count on Him to provide in unknown ways each year. And He always does.

THE FOCUS IS ON LIVES, NOT NUMBERS

"What do you think? If a man owns a hundred sheep, and one of them wanders away, will he not leave the ninety-nine on the hills and go to look for the one that wandered off?"

Matthew 18:12

In this verse, Jesus really illustrates well the principle of this chapter. That while even God casts a wide net, He is intimately interested in saving one at a time, and that if He only saved one, His heart would be just as thrilled as if He saved millions.

Someone once said, "A man's reach should exceed his grasp."

At Homes of Hope, we will never chase numbers at the expense of individuals. Our mission and calling is directed towards each individual, and we try to reach as many as we can, but we never reach so far as to exceed the grasp of the individual.

In the worlds of ministry, non-profit work, and for-profit business, the quest for scaling up is the same. If the ministry, work, product, or service is excellent and in high demand, there is societal, as well as internal, pressure put on the organization to scale it.

If we are just talking about widgets, maybe scale is a good thing. Indeed, scale is a good thing in ministry as well, to a point. But when we compare ourselves to Apple smart phones or Starbucks coffee, in terms of producing more, we make a critical mistake. We're not serving coffee. We're serving people.

And scale will not get the same results if the way you scale is to replicate exactly the same product or service to each person, like Apple and Starbucks do. Because in ministry, our clients each have a very unique and distinct story, chocked full of very unique and distinct circumstances, obstacles, and solutions.

An example of that is our decision around 2010 to scale back our Men's Workforce Development program from sixteen men to eight.

Many would see that as a concession or a failure, but we certainly didn't think it was either of those.

I knew in 2010 that I was being burdened about something in our Men's program, but not really sure what the burden was telling me to change. As I prayed and asked the Lord for direction, discernment, and wisdom, a direct answer didn't come immediately.

As a side note, many times in our lives, God will answer our question through an unexpected source. Sometimes a person, sometimes something written, but inevitably, something unexpected. I am so glad that I experienced these unexpected times, from unexpected source!

As I prayed about this burden, a coincidental comment came my way from Cyndi, our Comptroller, and fellow member of the Wilderness Group. As she was processing some kind of invoice, or something similar, relating to our Men's program, she remarked to me, "Don, sometimes it feels like the men are just workhorses."

That comment shook me to the core. Never once would I ever want anyone to think that we were using the men or taking advantage of them. Our program originally served eight men, but at that time we served sixteen. The way we had scaled up to sixteen was to utilize our men via lawn care. The men handled all the lawn care for all the rental housing that we owned.

We thought, *This is a great way to serve more men. We need lawn care anyway, and more men need our services. Let's do it.*

What it became though, was too many men for our staff to effectively serve with excellence, and in turn, we were just having more men in the program as a result.

So we stopped. We allowed several graduations to take place without replacement men, we weaned in outsourcing for lawn care until we eventually had only eight men in the program, and eventually had 100% of lawn care outsourced.

To this day, we have only increased the number of men to nine. We decided that less graduates with greater chances to succeed, was better than more graduates with only hopes for them to succeed.

And it was the right choice, without a doubt. Today, almost 100% of our graduates are still succeeding long after they leave our program. Before that, our success percentage, while still very good, was only 50-75%.

Scale to serve more is great, unless you are actually serving less.

A similar example, on the housing side of our ministry, was the decision to not build apartments.

In the early years, we were encouraged to compete for Low Income Housing Tax Credits (LIHTC) by many people. Today, it is, and has been for a long time, the single largest funding source to produce the largest number of affordable housing units in the United States.

Our problem though, was a reluctance to participate in that program, because it seemed that over 90% of the projects that received funding awards were for multi-story, multi-unit apartment buildings. And we simply did not want to warehouse people where income diversity was lacking, especially in a highly dense situation.

In fact, the vast majority of families that applied for our housing were trying to escape living situations just like that. So, while we could have probably developed 1,600 units of housing by now instead of 640 (at this writing), we simply would not have been fulfilling the calling that we received from the Lord.

There are many examples of this over the years. I remember one woman who came to us out of desperation, because a bullet had flown through her apartment window, and almost hit her young son simply doing his homework. Many stories of bad living situations have been told to us over the years that resulted from families crammed into apartment buildings that were not managed well. On a side note, there are indeed well managed apartment complexes that we know of and appreciate. We simply chose to pursue less dense development, for all the reasons this chapter explains.

Fear, and where you live, should not be codependents. This can be a by-product of chasing numbers.

Families we have served have found great success after we've housed them in single family community settings. This feeling of community comes from having their own front and back yard, their own front porch, their own security. And then allowing us to build relationships of trust with them, and they in turn with their neighbors. As they pursue economic mobility through things like budgeting and accessing banking services, or simply just starting their first savings account, this all becomes something tangible to them.

Many have taken their savings in housing costs and gone back to school to get a specialized education. which resulted in a better job and moving into greater economic mobility.

Many others have been able to qualify for home ownership after pursuing these connections to resources and financial wellness.

We like to say often that we want our clients to be the heroes of their own stories. What we mean by that is that empowerment should not be a commodity that we sell or give to them. If they have to come to us for empowerment every day, we become their power source. What we'd rather do is to create an atmosphere for empowerment wherein they empower themselves.

The Client Resources Department is a real and dedicated part of Homes of Hope. The staff wakes up every day thinking about how they can help connect clients to resources that they can utilize to empower themselves and become the heroes of their stories.

People want a chance, a level playing field. Real barriers exist for low-income people to access resources that more affluent folks take for granted. Connecting them to those resources can be life changing.

And when lives change like that, when doors are opened for economic mobility opportunities, and our clients walk through those doors and begin to reap the benefits, their children benefit, and then later on their grandchildren, and yes, true generational change happens. This is a beautiful thing.

All this has been possible because each family is served one at a- time. No warehousing. No number chasing.

The shepherd in Jesus' story (chapter scripture reference) is an example of the Great Shepherd who is our example in this guiding principle. Do not lose sight of the one, to serve the ninety-nine.

BEING STRATEGIC

"I am sending you out like sheep among wolves. Therefore, be as shrewd as snakes and as innocent as doves."

Matthew 10:16

I remember often saying over the years, "If there's one thing that I want to make sure everyone knows about our strategy, is that we have one." The founding principle of focus is really impossible without strategy.

That's not to say that strategies are the same as founding principles. Strategies can, and often should, change as the mission environment changes, or the needs of those you serve change. But strategies are as important as principles in terms of having them. They need each other.

A. WORKING WITH LOCAL GOVERNMENT

One strategy we employed early on was discovered, not decided on.

I remember speaking at an event after we had been recognized as successful in our work. A person in the audience stood up and complimented me for having such an effective track record for working with local governments across the state. To follow up his compliment, his question was, "So, how did you so effectively become partners with cities and counties? Is there some particular strategy you employed to connect with the mayors and council members, because I'm having a hard time doing it?"

I remember laughing at myself because I knew that we didn't employ any strategy at all in the beginning. I told him that we found by accident that working with community development staff personnel is much more effective, which led to interaction with politicians, because politicians, for the most part, trust the city or county staff personnel and will listen to them.

Being strategic sometimes is accidental at first. The key is to recognize it when it slaps you in the face, and make it your strategy.

I believe that many strategies actually should come accidentally if they are discovered while in pursuit of your mission. Because these discoveries would be based in reality and often would be led by the targets or objects of your strategy, learning from them what the best practices really are. Kind of an adaptive strategy model.

Local governments were no exception. In the early days, we actually learned a large portion of the execution of our housing mission from Ginny Stroud, the city of Greenville's Community Development Director. Ginny helped us navigate the complex world of Housing and Urban Development (HUD) grants and underwriting these grant applications. Ginny also connected us with consultants who helped us understand and execute this highly complex world of government funding.

By learning from these experts, we not only sharpened the tools on our workbench, but we created a strategy that worked when we decided to expand our housing footprint to other cities and counties.

B. HOUSING/WORKFORCE STRATEGIES

In a similar way, our housing strategies were also crafted after the boat was launched from the dock. Early on, we could plainly see that we wanted to meet the need for affordable housing, but we didn't know what the best practices were, and which ones would match our skills, passions, and geographic area, etc.

In a large way, our four housing strategies, along with our four strategies for helping the men in our Workforce Development program, came from listening and looking.

We listened to the needs by interjecting ourselves into the community conversations. We attended meetings that were held to address problems in the community specific to housing and workforce development, or addiction recovery. We also listened to those with resources.

No, we didn't chase the money, but we definitely listened to those willing to invest in the areas we were called. This is an example of this chapter's scripture reference about being shrewd.

Basically, I believe Jesus was saying this (my paraphrase):"Be very kind, trusting, loving and ethical when dealing with the business world. But also, be aware that it sometimes wants to devour you, so be prepared and on guard, and be very smart. Learn how it works and use that to the advantage of the Kingdom-building I've called you to do."

So listening to what those willing to invest in our work had to say, and learning their interests and motivations and processes, was critical to developing our strategies.

We also developed our strategies from looking. We observed what needs were already being addressed in the community, and which ones were not. We observed which ones needed more help and which ones were saturated.

From those observations, we saw where we could take our basic mission and inject it into these areas that needed more help. We used to say that we saw where Habitat for Humanity and others were serving well, and we focused on the areas they didn't focus on.

So, our four housing strategies became:

- Housing First:

Rental housing is a great way to allow a family to just breathe and get out of survival mode.

Families who need affordable housing are often paying 60-70% of their income for rent. Many are running through a cycle of evictions that result when any little unexpected extra expense was incurred, or when income was reduced, delayed, or temporarily eliminated.

In essence, we say, "Let's house you first, and then address other issues that can help you gain upward economic mobility and/or spiritual or emotional health."

By becoming their landlord, we have the unique ability to now build a relationship with them, and say, "Okay, you're out of crisis-mode, now let's talk about how we can help you beyond housing affordability." This obviously, as a Christ-centered ministry, gives us opportunity for discipleship. We share Christ's love with each family and work together with them on whatever areas He may already be working with them on, or introducing new areas they may not have recognized before.

Beyond Christian discipleship, when the family allows us to continue, we start with "The Three 'B's:'"Budgeting, Banking, Building assets.

Financial wellness we call it. This basic foundation of help beyond housing has been a great starting point for our staff to walk the road towards success with each family and see where each road leads. Anything less and we'll just be playing "musical chairs" with the same people.

Housing stability is crucial, but it must be a starting place not an ending place. Many of our clients see it as the end at first, but with relationships of trust being built, and Christian discipleship and financial wellness as a foundation, we can help them pursue their dreams, and move out of poverty cycles that have often kept them stuck. We call it generational change. Changed to the point of no return, their lives are so dramatically set on a new path that they teach their children and grandchildren these same things to insure asset growth for them as well.

On a separate but important note, this strategy also became critical to us in another way. Developing, then ultimately owning, rental housing enabled us (organizationally) to do the very thing we were encouraging our clients to do, which was to build assets.

And by building assets, this enabled our organization to grow and scale upward. With long-term sustainable organizational income, we have been able to develop more housing, increase and improve our programs, attract better employees, reach other markets, and be less reliant on donations and/or grants.

Housing First has definitely been a life-changing strategy both for the families housed, and for our organization, and has possibly been our most powerful one in terms of impact.

- Permanent Supportive housing:

This strategy was born out of both an inability, and an ability.

Our inability was that we couldn't effectively house homeless persons or families if they had no income. Now, we recognize that some homeless people or families do indeed have an income. For these, we can help. But for a homeless person with no income, they need an intermediary.

By that I mean an agency or a church that can take a person or family from zero income, through rehabilitation and programmatic efforts, to a place of stability and income. Many excellent organizations and churches do this very thing. But most of them do not offer what we call permanent housing, only temporary, which is understandable for many reasons.

These agencies needed permanent housing options for folks they'd helped and thus our "ability" created this second housing strategy. We know how to develop housing and are willing to own it permanently and rent it to people or families who need it.

And the additional key component for this, was an actual collaborative partnership with these other agencies, not just for referrals of people or families, but also for supportive services they would continue to offer to the folks housed, to insure the greatest chances for sustainable success.

- Home ownership gaps:

Our listening and looking also led us to discover this third housing strategy. It quickly became apparent that there was an underserved gap in the market that existed, for folks wanting to own homes. This gap existed in the lack of affordable housing for sale, for folks whose incomes were a bit over the qualifying "cut off line" for most HUD or similar programs. For them, most of the available housing stock in the market was unaffordable.

After observing through listening and looking, we decided to develop some of our homes for this market gap in home ownership, in addition to developing rental housing.

- LoCAL housing:

Spelled intentionally with the lower-cased 'o,' and pronounced like Low-Cal dressing, Lo-CAL Housing was the evolution of the original program of Homes of Hope. Originally, Homes of Hope renovated mobile homes and sold them to very low-income families for $5000, and we self-financed them to families at $100 per month, with 0% interest, resulting in fifty monthly payments.

This was a great start, and one to this day, is still the most economical program for affordable housing outside of just giving homes away, that we've ever encountered.

In fact, this program was fairly prolific in those early years, resulting in over one hundred homes that were developed in this way.

But something kept nagging at us. There were two inherent problems that this mobile home program could not solve. First, mobile homes would never be a real financial asset. Because they were classified in the same property assessment class as vehicles, their property assessment depreciated over time, like an automobile would. And secondly, no matter how well intentioned we were, and how hard we tried, making a mobile home energy efficient was an uphill battle, and one that was usually lost.

In fact, we discovered through listening and looking, that energy costs were sometimes three times the cost of the home. Imagine our disappointment when we heard that some of our housing recipients were paying $100 per month for their housing and $300 per month for their energy. We were frustrated.

Thus, we discovered another way that strategy is developed and that was through frustration.

Eventually, through more listening and looking, and very intentional thought and prayer, we found a solution to this problem. In the process, we solved another problem we didn't even think about.

We partnered with Joel Van Dyke, a principal at Freeman and Major Architects, to design a traditionally built home that would be highly energy efficient and still economical to build. We figured that if families we housed could afford $100 for their home payment and $300 for their energy, we would try to "flip" that financial model and find a way to build a home that they could afford for $300, and that would be energy efficient enough to lower their power bills to around $100.

And the effect would be a home that would actually appreciate in value and be a financial asset that could help the family grow out of poverty one day.

Thus was born LoCAL Housing. The acronym means:

- Long term
- Compact (the LoCAL home is a bit smaller than most)
- Affordable
- LEED standards (LEED is an energy-efficiency rating)

And the third problem that was solved in the process was that the level of training and skill that building traditionally built housing would benefit the men in our Workforce Development program.

A true win-win-win!

Similarly, we developed the four pillar strategies for our Men's Workforce Development program by using these same listening and looking methods.

Our core mission of Christian discipleship to men overcoming addictions never wavered. But these additional pillars that we wanted to build, that would hold up their new "house" (new life, attitude, skills, resources), became part of our strategies.

This new house each man graduates with is constructed like this:

- The foundation of Christ centered living.
- The four pillars of:
  » Marketable career skill
  » Affordable place to live after graduation
  » Affordable and reliable transportation after graduation
  » Education improvement
- The roof overhead consists of:
  » Soft-skills training
  » Financial education leading to economic mobility

These four pillars built over the foundation, plus the roof, became our strategies for producing good graduates with maximum chances of success after graduation.

We could never have ended up with such a well-constructed house without listening and looking.

C. FIRM MANAGEMENT

Lastly, our strategies demanded a closer look at management of rental housing that we developed and continued to own. And, not knowing anything about property management made this easy to follow the listen and look model.

The first thing we learned was how difficult it was to be a Christ-centered ministry simultaneous to being a landlord. This was very difficult.

We initially tried managing everything in-house but quickly discovered this was a bad idea. We then outsourced rent collections and most of the needed maintenance and repairs, so we could concentrate in-house on grant compliance, fair housing compliance and legal leasing compliance. We could also concentrate on the ministry part of building relationships of trust with each family.

We found that even though we outsourced rent collections and repairs, we still had to decide on our management philosophy so we could effectively communicate it to the property management companies we employed.

You can imagine the diversity of management philosophies that property management companies heard from their property owners. You can drive around town and look at the condition of certain properties and probably guess that some philosophies were actually non-existent.

Being Christ-centered, we defaulted to compassion, forgiveness, and multiple chances for our clients. And even today, all three of those attributes are present in our management philosophy. But we also discovered that more was needed.

Strong boundaries were needed in order to develop the communities we built, and we had to think of the neighborhood as a whole. Again, we learned this through listening and looking.

The communities our families were trying to escape were largely communities where bad behavior ran rampant. Local drug dealers hung out near kids' apartment complexes as the kids walked home from school, and gang members looking to recruit, were also commonplace. Even things like junky yards or porches, loud music, and more were tolerated as the norm.

We quickly learned that our communities needed strong and firm management.

I call it the Spiritual Star Trek principle.

One episode of Star Trek had Mr. Spock, the resident logical man from the logical planet Vulcan, sacrifice his life to save hundreds of others. In his dying comments, he said, "The needs of the many, outweigh the needs of the one."

While this is not always true, it is mostly true in community development.

We found that we had to heavily encourage our clients in being good neighbors if they wanted to have good neighborhoods. We said that if people wanted to practice bad behavior behind their closed doors, they had freedom to do that. But, if bad behavior came outside those closed doors onto their front porches or into the community, it was not acceptable. In those cases, we may not have been able to evict someone for being a bad neighbor, but we could choose to not renew their lease, and give somebody else a chance.

This has proven to be highly effective as the families we house are really wanting something better and the missing ingredient before was that no one made the effort to set boundaries in their communities. We felt that this was a must.

Occasionally, a family fooled us initially, but that didn't last past their annual lease renewal, and their neighbors noticed. And their neighbors appreciated it.

Strong and firm management may sound harsh, and sometimes it indeed is, but the needs of the many do, in this case, outweigh the needs of the one. This strong and firm management philosophy has been one we've stuck with and will continue to follow.

MEN'S WORKFORCE DEVELOPMENT

"All scripture is inspired by God and is useful to teach us what is true and to make us realize what is wrong in our lives. It corrects us when we are wrong and teaches us to do what is right. God uses it to prepare and equip His people to do every good work."

I Timothy 3:16-17 (New Living Translation/NLT)

Discipleship is still the foundation of everything we do. Matthew 25 teaches us to meet the needs of people in need. Matthew 28 teaches us to go and make disciples.

Our work in discipleship is very dependent on meeting the Matthew 25 needs first, so that those in need of Christ might be able to listen and receive.

Our Men's Workforce Development program was founded on this. Men who were literally homeless, on the street, and addicted to drugs or alcohol, aren't always eager to hear about Christ when they have no place to sleep, or are hungry and cold, and have irrational decision-making skills due to foreign substances in their bodies.

In the beginning, we were simply wanting to expose the men to some good influences, to some comradery, some accountability, and some opportunities to help others who may have even been less fortunate than they were. The skills that they learned renovating mobile homes were not very marketable, but we were satisfied that being clean and sober, with a new work ethic, work attitude, and outlook on life, with some life-skills thrown in, would be enough to launch them into some good second chances.

Over time, this grew into so much more. Today, our Men's Workforce Development graduates are employed with career-path jobs at above living-wage jobs with marketable skills that will command employment options and opportunities for the rest of their lives. Today our graduates are equipped as the scripture references, for successful lives. This includes all of the things we desired for them in the beginning, plus marketable skills, meaningful resources (their 4 pillars), and established social capital in the form of allies and connections in the community.

But there were some key lessons to be learned along the way, and some evolution of our programs and philosophies that needed to grow, and some that needed to transition.

A. Randy Green lesson

I call this the Randy Green (not his real name) lesson because Randy was the first man that we had to expel from our program. Boy was that hard. And today, anytime we have to do that, it is equally hard. It never gets easy. I guess I'm really glad that it doesn't.

But with that first expulsion, we learned a great deal that has kept us pursuing excellence in our program ever since.

While in our program, when Randy messed up and abused substances again, my natural default was to forgive with compassion and kindness. We loved Randy. Randy was a great guy and the nicest guy you'd ever want to meet.

But I was fortunate enough to have Winn Freeman, the founder of the Overcomer's program at Miracle Hill Rescue Mission, as an ally in those early days. He knew far more about working with men overcoming addictions that we did.

Winn knew Randy. In fact, if I remember correctly, Randy was a graduate of Winn's program. But when I asked Winn's advice, he said, "Don, God is a big God, and He doesn't need you guys to save everybody. God has got Randy, and He'll take care of Randy. But you owe it to the other men in the program to not let him stay. Accountability is the most missing thing in their lives and it's the reason a lot of them got where they are. You have to release Randy to God and let God keep him, and you have to show those other men in the program their value in the process." I have never forgotten his words.

It was hard advice, but really, really good advice. And to this day, we think about Winn's words when confronted with a similar situation. His advice continues to be confirmed as Spirit led indeed, and transformational.

I can't tell you how Randy turned out. I unfortunately lost touch. I hope that he's okay. I can tell you though, that as of this writing, out of the 316 other men who have graduated our program, the great majority have turned out really, really great. I hope that Randy did too.

B. Dramatic transition

The other things that made a dramatic transition in our Men's Workforce Development program came with a change in leadership and a new partnership.

Steve Vicari came to us as our new Director of Men's Workforce Development in 2012. Steve is actually a graduate of our program, as he found us in the midst of his own life struggle with addiction. Steve was, and is, a gifted preacher of the Word, and was a successful pastor before drugs got in his way.

During Steve's time with us in his recovery, he so impressed us that we created a job for him so he could stay on after graduation. This was not our norm at all, and one of only a few times that we had done this, but Steve had a special calling on his life, and we recognized it.

Shortly after that though, our friends at Miracle Hill Ministries also recognized that call and asked permission to discuss hiring him as their Director of Transitions. We gladly recognized God's call to that for Steve and blessed his leaving with joyful sadness.

About five years later, when the time came for us to hire a new director of Men's Workforce Development, I gave Miracle Hill the same courtesy and asked permission to try and recruit Steve back. And back he came!

This new leadership was transformational in having a fresh set of spiritual eyes and ears overseeing this program, and many improvements began to happen.

On a side note, I know that this same transformation will also happen when someone follows my time at Homes of Hope. I look forward to seeing that, for it will be great indeed. But I am in no rush.

The other transformation was our partnership with Greenville Technical Collage.

This partnership added something we'd never had before with Men's Workforce Development, which was outside credentials. We'd always graduated our men with credentials from us, but this was new and powerful.

Having certifications of accredited trainings and classes certified by Greenville Tech was game changing for our graduates. It took their accomplishments to another level. Not only could they tell potential employers of their new skills, now they could also layer these with credentials of safety training and work skills training.

And by the way, our partnership with Greenville Tech has been great for both partners. In fact, I'd like to share this story and following email between the overseer of our partnership at Greenville Tech, and our Men's Program director, Steve.

> The Greenville Tech Director had emailed the main classroom instructor this question: "Are there any issues with the Homes of Hope program that I should know about? I'm about to check in with Steve Vicari at Homes of Hope and wanted to tell him if there are any."

Here is the instructor's reply:

> "The only issue with the Homes of Hope men is they make all our other students look lazy and unmotivated. As an instructor, they spoil you because they are such great students. These guys are a real pleasure to work with. And you can also see the difference in the Electrical classes between the guys from Homes of Hope, and those that are not from Homes of Hope."

Wow! This warmed our hearts to hear about the attitudes of our men, and to hear that in the midst of their own training and life change, they are also providing blessing to Greenville Tech.

Ever since this partnership was added to our program, 100% of our graduates have been hired after completing our program, and hired at very good starting wages that set them on career paths for growth! This was, and continues to be, so exciting for them and us.

C. New facility

The third transformation for the Men's Workforce Development program was a brand-new Training Center we opened and dedicated in our twentieth year.

This Training Center was purchased for us by Golf-for-Greenville, a philanthropic fundraising event of Fluor Corporation, who is and has been one of our top partners in this work!

This new facility gave the Men's Workforce Development program something it lacked over the previous twenty years, a visibility in the community. Before, their training space was in the back part of our ministry offices without a sign or any visibility from the road, unless you knew it was there.

This new facility gave them great exposure in the community, but it also gave them top quality training space. The space included a smart-board for classroom training, a modern new classroom, offices for the Men's Workforce Development staff, and a huge shop space for a carpentry shop, and work-stations for each man. In the middle of the space was a completely framed-up LoCAL house for them to practice on when the weather is bad or if they are in between builds.

We believe this most recent transformational improvement may have the biggest impact of them all. Truly, God is working mightily in this program and lives are being changed.

To close, I'd like to share a success story from the Men's Workforce Development Program. There are over three hundred of these stories and so telling only one seems insufficient—but this chapter would not be complete without at least sharing one.

Brett Porter is our Community Relations Director, who was also a graduate of our Men's Workforce Development Program. He has written the below story about John, who was in the program when Brett was.

"John was a convicted felon with a horrible attitude (which was ironic because he always wore a hat that said attitude is everything). He almost flunked his senior year of high school, had numerous failed attempts at college and countless run-ins with the law. To say he had little going for him would be an understatement.

Where does someone like John go to get help? Jail didn't work and rehab seemed to depress him even more. He was two weeks away from graduating a seventh month inpatient treatment center when he realized he needed something more. This is where his Homes of Hope story began.

When John arrived at Homes of Hope he was still on the fence. Still breaking rules and putting forth very little effort to change. He was the doom and gloom Eeyore of the bunch that some thought would never amount to anything. For John to change, it would truly take a miracle.

Mornings came early at Homes of Hope. Devotion began at 6:30 a.m. and would usually start with praise and worship before diving into a heartfelt message from the director. He would preach for an hour, and then everyone would break for work. John was very apathetic towards both. Preaching...ugh, and work...double ugh.

Work involved residential construction while also being mentored by two veteran staff members. Both men had walked the hard road of addiction and were well equipped to lead the next generation of men through the recovery process.

This is exactly what John needed. Daily discipleship from men who cared while learning a skilled trade began to birth purpose in his life.

Change was slow but it wasn't long before John uttered the words "I think I'm right where God wants me." These were big words coming from a man who was once very skeptical of Christianity, even strongly opposing/mocking it at times.

I went from doing everything in my power to avoid him, to staying up late listening to him share and speculate about what God was up to in his life. What in the world was happening and how was it happening?

I began to witness John take advantage of the opportunities placed before him. He began to engage at the devotion table in the mornings, work through his doubts and strain to believe that God had plans for him.

After nine months of being in the program, it was time for John to get a job. At this point he had been part of the building and completion of four homes. Through this process, he developed framing and electrical skills that landed him a job with an electrical contractor.

He purchased his first vehicle outright, was released from probation, and became a registered voter for the first time in ten years. He then furthered his education at Greenville Tech and received a full pardon of fourteen felonies.

Today, John owns his very own electrical business and is going to bible college."

WORKING MORE FERTILE LAND

CULTURE SHIFTS AND CORPORATE BONES

"Now I commit you to God and to the word of His grace, which can build you up and give you an inheritance among all those who are sanctified."

Acts 20:32

In the process of gaining experience over the early years, we also realized that chronology alone did not always automatically produce wisdom, nor avoid stagnation.

After a few seasons of pursuing excellence and focusing on the principles that God had taught us, some weaknesses became obvious, and some challenges to grow, became more glaring.

Success is fertile ground for blindness, and can lead to overlooking weaknesses and necessity to change. Accolades and achievements are barriers to growth because they feel good and give us pride in ourselves, which can become blinders. We overlook, because we do not see.

A spirit of excellence demands that you always grow. Not in size, or quantity of output, but in quality. Quality of operations, programs, design, practicality, and viewpoints, to name a few. We constantly challenge our staff and board, and even our volunteers to strive for growth in these areas that will result in stronger ministry, stronger organization, stronger corporate bones.

An example of the need for growth, in fact, a culture shift, is detailed in the chapter about our Men's Workforce Development program when leadership changed.

Culture shifts are dramatic because culture is almost akin to the air we breathe. It is everything, because it is like air, in that we cannot survive without it. It is the way we operate, our norms, our lives. And so, a shift can cause us to stop breathing for a minute, to gasp for air, to even turn blue.

And leading through a culture shift is hard. It requires a lot of determination and two-way trust. Many companies, ministries, churches, etc., have not survived culture shifts. They simply could not breathe. And even the ones who did not die, died in other ways when they went back to their old air.

Recognizing the need for a culture shift takes great courage and trust in the leader, not the human one but the God one. He is able to lead culture shifts because He has done it. Read the Bible: stories of culture shifts are all through it.

People don't like breathing new air. They get tired and frustrated. It is hard but it is worth it.

Another example of a culture shift at Homes of Hope came through recognizing our need to build staff and board capacity. As our output in the community, even statewide, and our impact grew, we saw the need to strengthen our corporate bones.

This manifests in some scary landscapes. Hiring new staff who didn't always line up with our worldview was scary. From a budgeting standpoint, paying market wages to attract more talented staff was scary. Developing our board to attract people who would never be satisfied if the board were just a rubber-stamp group, was scary.

Yet we knew that we had to do these things if we wanted to grow and strengthen our corporate bones. And we were motivated to do them because the mission would be served better because of them.

Over the years, this courage to shift the culture and strengthen our bones has paid off exponentially. Our staff is operating at a level of excellence we couldn't have imagined before. Our Board of Directors is operating as a governing board, using the accepted best practices for non-profit boards and functioning at the highest level in our history. Even our volunteers go through training and have policies and procedures and operate with unbelievable efficiency and impact.

Growth is a best practice with us. Our Chief Operating Officer, Dawn Dowden, always tells the staff and board, "If you are opposed to growing as a person in your role here, you really don't need to be here." Quite a challenge and a very healthy one at that!

The spirit of excellence is not pursuit of perfection; it is the pursuit of improvement. We shouldn't be afraid to shift the air being breathed or rattle the bones of structure in an effort to strengthen them.

BALANCE OF COMMUNITY AND ECONOMIC DEVELOPMENT

"Finally, all of you, be like-minded, be sympathetic, love one another, be compassionate and humble."

1 Peter 3:8

Over the years our mission never really changed but the way we pursued it surely did.

In the beginning, our initial mission statement was, "We rebuild homes for low-income families or individuals, while also providing job training/mentoring for men overcoming addictions." Our vision tagline was, "It's not just about houses, it's about lives."

Today, our mission statement is, "We open doors for economic mobility through housing, economic, and workforce development." And our Vision Statement is, "Generational change throughout South Carolina."

Of course, I like the current ones better, but even the first one reflected that we wanted to pursue more than just Matthew 25 help for folks, but also to *"Go and make disciples,"* (Matthew 28), and to also help folks beyond housing and/or job training. To impact them to a point of no return, where not only their lives are impacted, but their children's and grandchildren's lives are too, affecting generations to come.

As these statements evolved so did our understanding of the problems we wanted to help solve, and the people who we served, and the ways best to help. We learned the complexities of community and economic development and that the two are inseparable.

We learned that there were unintended negative consequences that occurred as a result of our work in housing, like gentrification and rising property taxes.

We learned the importance of energy affordability, not just housing affordability.

We learned the importance of affordable housing being market quality. It's hard enough being low-income without your house looking like crap.

We learned the need for economic education and connections to economic resources, which should lead to economic mobility. We learned that this is not something you just hand to someone in a pamphlet. We learned that building relationships of trust, over time, was the only way to connect to this need.

We learned that just because someone was poor or low-income, didn't mean we should make assumptions. We sometimes assume that there are two people in life that low-income people do not know. We assume they don't know Jesus, and we assume they don't know "jack." Both assumptions are often untrue.

We learned that asset growth is the most critical missing financial element keeping families in poverty, and that there were, and are, many, many barriers (especially for people of color) to this asset growth.

We learned the importance of community, not just development, which led to decisions about our homes all having nice front porches so neighbors could more easily interact with each other, and placing our homes close to the front sidewalk when possible so conversations with neighbors could be easier.

We learned the importance of removing dead-end streets from communities where bad activities tended to happen under-cover at these dead ends.

We learned the importance of having a diversity of income ranges living together in neighborhoods to encourage sharing not just of a cup of sugar, but each other's social capital. Sharing connections to people, resources, services, jobs, etc.

We learned how to strategically place senior citizens nearby young families to encourage the passing along of chronological wisdom as well as enhancing the opportunity for younger energy helping older bones occasionally.

We learned the critical importance of job skills, not just work skills. We learned that men who overcame addictions were still not getting good paying jobs after graduation simply because they had a new work ethic and attitude and were clean and sober. We learned that employers wanted soft skills to accompany job skills and that they were willing to pay when skills came along with sobriety.

We learned that our success rate for our men graduates went from near 75% (still very good) to almost 100% when these skills were added to their sobriety.

We learned that gentrification was a powerful force. One that was way stronger than we'd ever anticipated. In fact, we didn't anticipate it at all in the beginning. And once anticipated, we learned it was a worthy foe.

And on a side note, and to expand on that topic, we also learned to start talking about something that is called Gentrification with Justice. This being that if gentrification was going to happen and we couldn't stop it, it should at least happen with justice. And we could be a part of the education of those gentrifying.

Gentrification with Justice means four things:

- Let's not overbuild. Build a home more in keeping with the sizes and character of the surrounding homes in the neighborhood.

- Be a neighbor. Don't immediately hide behind a privacy fence and pull down the shades. Get to know the new neighbors.

- Go to neighborhood gatherings—especially Neighborhood Association meetings. And remember that the neighbors were here first, so listen well.

- Share your social capital. It is the thing we have that low-income neighbors want the most. Not our bigger houses or newer cars or even our bank accounts. Social capital connects people to opportunity and resources. All our neighbors want is a fighting chance to better themselves.

A great example of this is the neighborhood we developed called Chicora Crest in Greenville.

Doubters were often present when we described our vision for Chicora Crest. The idea of mixed income housing being still very new in Greenville in 2007 emboldened the doubters, but we were determined that it would work. In the end, we developed twenty-nine homes there, a little more than half of them were sold as market rate homes, and the rest are rented to low-income families.

And gentrification with justice happened.

Today, those neighbors enjoy living together so much that they raised their own funds to construct a community garden on one of the green spaces provided in the neighborhood. Later, they raised more money, themselves, to construct a gazebo on another green space in the neighborhood, so they could have a place to socialize together. They even celebrate birthdays together there each month! What a beautiful community it is.

All these things we have learned in the pursuit of community and economic development. Each thing needs the other. They are indeed inseparable.

INNOVATION IN FINANCE

"But the helper, the Holy Spirit, whom the Father will send in my name, He will teach you all things and bring to your remembrance all that I have said to you."

John 14:26

Sometimes ministries struggle because of a lack of financial expertise and innovation.

We have however, often been complimented for our innovation, especially in finance. But God is the smart one here, and our innovation is not difficult for Him. He has never once scratched His head and said, "You know, I'm not sure what to do about Homes of Hope's problems."

One of the early things we learned was how to leverage. HUD is actually effective (I can't believe I just said that) in requiring that those who receive their grants and loans must leverage them with other dollars, usually private funds, so that their funds can accomplish more.

This is a good policy for governmental funding. Many don't know about this, but I give credit here where it is due and that goes to HUD. And it is powerful.

Oh, but by the way, Jesus was actually way ahead of HUD. He is the author of leveraging. Remember the five loaves and two fish?

So, through learning this, we learned that it doesn't have to be governmental funds that you leverage. Private capital, market profits, tax credits, even investment can be leveraged to accomplish greater things.

And, we also learned that we don't have to look to all sources, or even the same sources, for each need in financing the work.

For example, in housing, the cost to buy land, develop it, and then build on it usually costs the same for us as it does for market builder/developers. Sometimes we are fortunate enough to receive donated land or materials, but not as often as the general public thinks. Usually, we have to make housing affordable with cheap money, not cheap materials, or cheap labor.

To explain further, let's use an example of a house costing $100,000 to build. If we simply went to the local bank and borrowed $100,000, we'd have to sell the house to our targeted low-income family for $100,000 because we have to pay the bank back.

In this example, the buyer cannot afford to pay $100,000. Let's say they can afford $70,000 because of their low-income.

Now we have to find $30,000 somewhere that we do not have to pay back, (borrowing only $70,000 now from the bank) meaning that the purchasing family only has to pay $70,000 for the home, because that's the cost passed forward to the end user, i.e., the amount we have to pay back the bank.

Likewise, if we rented the house to our target low-income family, the rent to cover a $100,000 loan to us as the house owner/landlord would be, let's say, $1,200 per month.

Our family can only afford $600. So again, we have to find some low (or no) cost money, to pass on the lower loan cost to our renters and enable them to pay $600 rent.

Please note: these calculations are for illustration purposes only. The actual financial situations, rates, and calculations vary.

So when we have an opportunity to develop a site for housing, we look for the sources of funds that are low (or no) cost. Government grants are certainly at the top of this list because of its abundance, but over the years that abundance has dwindled greatly.

So we look at other sources. Obviously most non-profits default to donated funds, but let me just say that this default, if it is the only source pursued, is why so many non-profits produce small results. Donated funds are limited to the capacity and willingness of donors and are not easily obtained. After all, the donor receives nothing in return financially except a tax deduction (in most cases), and non-financially in the form of a social impact, which we always hope is enough to incent them to donate.

But innovation demands that we continue to look and not settle on the old way of doing it as the sole source.

We may look to tax credits that are available for us to sell to investors who pay income taxes (we, as a non-profit, do not pay income taxes) and in exchange for the credits we receive their capital, that we then invest into the home, and thus do not have to pass along any costs to our end user who is our low-income family.

Or we may decide that the regular market is strong and the area not gentrifying, and we build a market rate home next door or nearby. Then we would sell it at a reasonable profit, pushing that profit over onto the affordable house next door, or nearby. This profit then becomes the form of funds we invest in that house that we don't have to repay, which lowers our end user's cost to buy/rent.

For another example, we may offer our donors the opportunity to invest instead of donating. This could be money invested into our rental housing at a very low interest rate where the payment is deferred for ten years, thus enabling us to season our housing over the ten years through property appreciation and debt reduction. That, in turn would allow us to repay our investor at the end of ten years through refinancing the loan.

Being financially innovative isn't limited to housing, as we should also be innovative in managing our own corporate finances, but it is the most prominent area where this is evident.

And besides wanting to increase our output by being innovative, we particularly love sharing these things in the hopes that it stirs other non-profits, ministries, and churches to think entrepreneurially too, and be innovative.

God is the author of innovation and the source of any that we claim, so I know He is very willing to share with others who will seek His financial leadership too. *"Behold, I am doing a new thing."* (Isaiah 43:19)

PART III

FINISH WELL AND PASS THE BATON

Part III communicates some closing thoughts that sometimes dominate my thinking as I face the winter of my time leading Homes of Hope.

STILL DESPERATE

THE POOR ARE WITH YOU

*"The poor you will always have with you,
but you will not always have Me."*

Matthew 26:11

First let me just say that the majority of folks I know who are poor in pocketbook are some of the richest in sprit. And the most dignified.

I just wanted to get that settled.

Now, one of the most quoted verses among ministries that serve those with lower incomes, or no incomes, is Matthew 26:11 above. Over the years, I have found it frustrating though, because usually only the first half of the verse is quoted, and it is often quoted as a statement of resignation. We resign ourselves to the fact that the poor will always be with us because Jesus said they would. And we often also resign to less than maximum efforts on their behalf.

This statement by Jesus was in the context of the story about the woman who anointed His feet and the complaints that came as a result. That this was a waste of expensive ointment, especially in relation to so many poor people who were in need, and who could have benefited from the sale of this ointment. Instead, the woman worshiped Jesus with it.

He rightly pointed out that the poor will always be in our midst, but that He would not, at least not in human form. And, while the context accurately portrays this, often, only the first part of the verse if quoted.

"The poor you will always have with you."

So we settle into this statement as fact and we work to alleviate poverty knowing all along that poverty will not be eradicated, because Jesus said so.

This has always bothered me. Jesus was making a point about the importance of worshiping God above all other things, even noble and important things like helping the poor. And I don't believe He intended for the first part of the statement to be one of resignation towards the poor. But that is what it has become.

Jesus often told stories we call parables, and He often used these stories to teach the people. He also preached and made statements like this verse to make a point. Sometimes He asked questions of the people to test their faith or expose their priorities. And sometimes, He issued commands to be followed.

So what if we looked at this verse as a command instead of a statement?

Think about being in a crowded room and someone comes up to you and asks this: "Who are you with?" You immediately say, "I'm with that group over there," or, "I'm with that person in the corner." You are identified by who you are with.

What if we heard the verse this way? Would it change our perspective on our work and interaction with the poor? If we saw it as a command to always identify ourselves as being with the poor, would it change things?

I think it would drastically change things.

Emmanuel, God is with us. His very name implies that He thinks this way about us. He identifies with us. He is always with us. In the same way, we should identify with the poor. For He also said, "When you've done it unto the least of these, you've done it unto Me." (Matthew 25:45)

When we identify with the poor, we identify with Christ. Someone said working among the poor is our training ground for heaven. But there is even more to it. Simply working among the poor isn't what Christ meant in the scripture reference. I believe He wants us to be with them, and they with us. We have each other's backs. We are identified with each other.

So, how do we do that?

One thing I've found helpful is to listen. Not just hear, but listen. Beyond words.

All people, but especially low-income or homeless people, when in situations where they think you are about to help them, often tell you what they think you want to hear. It is human nature. But if you are indeed with them, you will listen beyond their words to see what it is that they are really telling you.

For example, at Christmas time, you are working with a client family in poverty, asking what things you can put on their list for gifts from the local community exchange. During your conversation, their teenage son blurts out, "I want video games!"

It would be easy to lecture the young man on being more practical and focusing his energy on more productive things. But, if you are truly with that family, while identifying with them and listening beyond their words, you may dig a bit deeper. You find that what the young man is really saying beyond his words is, "I really need to be challenged."

We get this idea that because people are poor their wants and needs are different than everyone else's. I once heard a speaker who said she interviewed people on a middle-class street and asked them what their greatest desires were for their neighborhood. The answers included: being safe, having neighbors you could count on, having walkable space to interact and exercise, and having a nice home.

These are the same things that most people of lower incomes want for their neighborhoods. Why do we think it would be different?

We think it is different because we have resigned ourselves to the fact in the scripture that says the poor you will always have with you. Therefore, they must be resigned to hopes and dreams that are less than, or different than ours.

But sometimes the poor just want the status quo too.

Currently, as I write this, there is a homeless man who almost daily passes through the neighborhood where our corporate offices are located. His name is Frank.

Frank seems to want to stay homeless, as some choose to do, as he has usually rejected repeated help when offered.

Frank has a cell phone. Almost daily Frank stops by and sits down on the pine straw near some of our shrubs, next to where our outside electrical outlet is. Frank charges his cell phone there. Frank also sometimes uses our shrub for his urinal.

Frank seems like a nice guy overall. We've offered him help, but he has always politely declined. Seemingly, he doesn't mind being homeless and he appears fairly happy.

I thought about Matthew 25:45 above the other day when I waved at Frank, as I pulled out of the parking lot. I thought, *That's Jesus over there charging His cell phone.* Well, it kind of is, isn't it?

If we do it unto the least of these knowing it is the same thing as doing it unto Him, what's the difference?

We have no problem identifying with Christ. He is our Lord and savior and He died for us and He is preparing our room in heaven. Why though, do we have problems identifying with Frank?

Jim Cymbala, the pastor of the Brooklyn Tabernacle Church in New York City, tells the story of a time when he was spiritually drained, but learned a good lesson. Pastor Cymbala's church is famous for its work with the homeless and poor, and was located right in what is called a difficult area of the city.

One Sunday night, after preaching in multiple services during the day, Jim was especially tired and drained, and was ready for a bit less stressful night service. Frankly speaking, he was ready to just go home and lie down.

While he was talking to the congregation from the front, a homeless man wandered in. Jim was used to this, so he didn't think much about it, and so he just kept talking.

Usually, a homeless person would find a seat during the service and ask for help at the end. But this night, this man didn't do that. He kept walking towards Jim and only stopped about five steps from Jim, just looking at him. Jim could tell that the man wanted to speak with him, right there in front of everyone.

Jim, being exhausted, decided not to ask the man to take a seat. Instead, to expedite matters, Jim simply held out a five-dollar bill and offered it to the man, thinking, *Let's just cut to the chase here.* But the man didn't take the bill. In fact, he slapped at Jim's hand pushing the bill away.

The man said, "I don't want your money, I want the Jesus I heard you talking about." It broke Jim that day. Weeping, he embraced the man and led him to Jesus, but he said that he realized that day that he needed Jesus more than the homeless man did at that moment.

We make assumptions about the poor sometimes because we don't identify with them. We make assumptions based on them being so different than us. We make assumptions based on our resignations that the poor will always be around.

But will we always be with them?

"Who are you with?" I'm with them, and they are with me.

RENEWED FAITH, RENEWED FIGHT

"Even youths grow tired and weary, and young men stumble and fall; but those who hope in the Lord will renew their strength. They will soar on wings like eagles; they will run and not grow weary, they will walk and not be faint."

Isaiah 40:30-31

When I turned fifty-seven, I did a math equation to evaluate my life. You, who hate math, please bear with me now. One of my few skills apparently is numbers, so this is how I think sometimes.

Realizing that I was thirteen years away from my desired retirement age of seventy, I also thought about how old I was when I began working. I was just less than eighteen.

Further doing the math, I realized that my projection of working until seventy years old, worked out to be a fifty-two-year working career.

I also knew that there were fifty-two cards in a deck, because there are four suits in a deck, thirteen cards per suit. Apparently another of my skills is cards I guess.

Similarly, there are fifty-two weeks in a year, and four seasons of thirteen weeks each. Anyway, you get the picture.

So, I realized that I had finished three of my thirteen year seasons of my working career, making the one ahead of me my winter.

Further thinking led me to evaluate what each season had taught me. Here is what I learned:

- Spring (ages 18-31)—began my working career, but ended with failure as I had worked my way all the way up to my dream of owning my own business only to fail at it, and having to close it.
- Summer (ages 31-44)—regrouping from that loss led me to eventually find my life calling to Homes of Hope, but after our year one funding was lost, I found myself at forty-four, right in the midst of our wilderness period.
- Fall (ages 44-57)—coming through the wilderness successfully and finding success at Homes of Hope beyond anything I'd ever imagined.
- Winter (ages 57-70) (if I make it)—asking myself what the final thirteen-year season would look like and asking God for wisdom in how to finish the race.

At this writing I am sixty-two.

Seeking His wisdom, I felt that the Lord showed me three themes at each season transition. Here they are:

- First season change—I had failed at the one thing I was good at—business. But looking back, I knew that I had not relied on my faith like I would have liked (in hindsight) to have. I had relied too heavily on myself. And I think I gave up too easily too. I could have worked harder.
  - » God showed me that this was my time of "No faith, no fight."

- Second season change—here I was in the midst of the wilderness, but just about to come out of it. Coming through the wilderness strengthened me like nothing ever had before, or has since. I grew closer to God and learned more about myself than ever, and truly found a faith that not just believed God could, but believed God would.
    - God showed me that this was my time of "Great faith, great fight."
- Now I found myself at the last season transition. What was my theme for it? Would I have to wait till the end to find out? Perhaps. But in seeking His wisdom, I believed that God was showing me.
    - I believe that this will be my time of "Renewed faith, renewed fight."

So I concluded that God was simply telling me that I was to finish strong with renewed fervency to stand in faith and fight for the calling and mission and the impact that He'd called us to achieve. I felt good. I could do this! What a great finish!

Oops.

I was wrong.

For a while I kept wrestling with this. I was wrestling and I was restless. I had no peace about this new theme. The Lord had His finger on something and I wasn't sure what. But I knew what His finger felt like. It's a loving pressure, but it was pressure just the same. I had gotten it wrong somehow.

I began an intense period of prayer over several weeks, so I could have peace for my final work season. What was the theme of my winter? I really wanted to get that right and finish well. I really wanted to lead Homes of Hope in the way the Lord wanted me to, and hand the baton off to a sprinting runner in full stride.

Finally I understood. The words were correct, but the application was wrong. Indeed I was to work with renewed faith and renewed fight, but not just for the mission, but also for my role.

I was to renew my faith in God alone being the Chief Executive Officer (CEO) of Homes of Hope, and not me. I was to renew my faith in God alone to do the work and fulfill the mission. I was to renew my faith at the level it was in the wilderness when I felt completely helpless and completely relied on Him.

That was the easy part. Although it will not be easy, as success brings complacency and comfort, as well as pride and arrogance and ego, but compared to the second part of the theme, this will be the easy part.

The second part was that I have to renew my fight. But not with long hours working, or even long hours praying, or willingness to take risks and have courage. No, this fight was to be done with myself. My ego. I was instructed to fight it, and slay it.

Be careful what you try to slay. It just might kill you first.

In the final season of my working career, my "winter," I am to fight hard to empower others to lead, and for them to eventually take my place, and to celebrate them. I am to fight hard to not be guilty of hanging onto the way to do it when younger smarter people just may have a better way. I am to fight hard to allow them to make their own mistakes and support them when they do, without an "I told you so."

I am to fight hard to support the organization and its leaders from a less visible place. To teach others what I have learned but without getting the credit, and with subtlety, without them even knowing that I am teaching them.

I am to slay my own ego by fighting it, and have great renewed faith for a better Homes of Hope beyond me. I am to do this with all my might.

My winter will be challenging, but I am determined to finish strong and pass the baton to a sprinter in full stride.

God is the CEO, not me. Apart from Him, I can do nothing. (John 15:5).

EVEN MORE DESPERATE

"Trust in the Lord with all your heart and lean not on your own understanding."

Proverbs 3:5

To conclude this book, I only have left one thing to do. To re-present this critical theme, and recommend it to you, or your organization, that it has been the most life-changing theme to try and live out myself.

Living through the wilderness was my greatest privilege, and perhaps my greatest triumph, even though I did nothing and He did everything. In it, I learned to never again be afraid, and that God is real, and that He can be trusted.

I also claim two other sureties; that are so valuable in a life full of un-surety. One, God loves us all, and two, His word is true. These things I am certain of.

The theme of the book is to be "Still desperate, even in the Promised Land."

I've touched on it already, but it is founded in the thought that wilderness desperation is easy. In the wilderness, all I had to do was wake up every morning, open my arms to heaven, and manna fell down.

But promised land desperation is harder. Because the land flows with milk and honey and the Lord gives it to us to work and till and produce, and thus prosper.

But to be desperate in prosperity? It doesn't make any sense.

In prosperity there is much more at stake. More lives impacted and more in need looking to us for help. And we are more desperate because the work is more complex. Given our growth and the innovation of our work, and the level of expectations we put on ourselves, and our clients put on us, we are more lost than ever before if left to our own wisdom and abilities. We need God now more than ever.

Please never lose sight of this great truth. God will give you all the freedom in the world to trust Him and pursue your calling, but if you do it depending on yourself you will fail. We are broken people, and short of heaven we cannot do anything by ourselves. (John 15:5 again)

By all means, live in His promised land, but be desperate, so desperate, for Him.

ACKNOWLEDGEMENTS

To Tim Revis—without whom this story would not have been. His obedience to the Lord via a dream in the middle of the night, inspired by a tremendous need that he was compelled to try and meet, was the birth of Homes of Hope. Thousands of people have him to thank for their improved lives.

To the wilderness group—Cyndi Gullick, Ted Cochran, Nate Fleming, Bob Ivins, and Keith Hundley. Although this book is the Homes of Hope story which encompasses many, your faith and dedication during the wilderness, just like Tim, is also the reason Homes of Hope exists.

To our Chief Operating Officer, Dawn Dowden—you have taught me many things, including, but not limited to: the critical importance of strong corporate bones and staff and board capacity; the critical importance of best practices and fiscal discipline; the critical importance of board and donor education; and by observation but most of all, how to lead with great love, your Homes of Hope family. We would not be the success we are today without you.

To all of our Board of Directors over the years—your leadership and commitment to give and to provide fiscal and organizational oversight is amazing, especially knowing that all of you have important other causes and businesses to pay attention to. I tell each year's Board that they are my all-time favorite. Well, I'm telling the truth each time! You guys are awesome!

To Brett Pyle—who graciously penned the foreword for this book, but who also, as my CEO coach over many years has challenged me like few ever have and has caused me to question my answers many times. His coaching always pointed me to Christ and His will and plan. I am forever grateful for you Brett.

To Ginny Stroud, the former Community Development Director, City of Greenville—your help and support literally taught us in the early years. Your willingness to take a chance on a small non-profit who repaired trailers with homeless men's help, was quite extraordinary, and is one I am eternally grateful for. You'll probably never know how much credit you deserve for our success, but you deserve a lot.

To the late Charlie Warth—you were my very good friend and you taught me so much. Your wisdom for this work was exceeded only by your heart for it. I miss you every day.

To those wonderful ladies who worked in our Thrift store all those years ago especially Pat Odom who ran the store. Though we only had the store for a few years, it provided something very critical to us during the wilderness, a little cash flow to help pay the bills.

To every lender over the years who helped to finance our housing developments—your friendships have been my favorite part of our journey together, but I'll have to say, your capital investments were pretty cool too.

To Bernie Mazyck, CEO of South Carolina Association for Community Economic Development or SCACED—you inspired me in 2005 when I first met you and heard you speak. I'm in awe of you and your work, and your members. They are amazing. Your friendship and leadership in the movement of community and economic development continues to inspire me. And teach me.

And I still think you're a cross between Jesus Christ, Martin Luther King, and Don Cornelius.

To Reid Lehman and Miracle Hill Ministries—if you hadn't bought into Tim's crazy idea in 1998, this likely wouldn't have happened. Thank you for valuing the men in your shelter and their need for more, and their desire to succeed in life.

To Julia Boland—who's keen perception caused me to revise a part of this book so that greater clarity would be brought to the reader, in a critically important area of our story.

To Dallas Burnett—for your persistent encouragement to finish the work of this book. Thanks for always pushing me towards that goal.

To all of our other partners in non-profit work—many of you are actual partners in serving with us directly, and our work together brings us great satisfaction and joy, and learning by watching, but even those who are not direct partners, we consider you all partners in the calling to help those in need. I salute you!

To all of the corporations who have sponsored our work—you have done so much to advance the cause and help us accomplish the work! Your generosity and willingness to volunteer and donate simply astonish me!

To the faithful employers who have hired our Men's Program graduates over the years—you cannot know how much this has been appreciated! Giving these men a chance to succeed is seen by many as a great risk, but you have proven willing to overlook that and invest into their lives. These men are grateful, and so are we.

To all the vendors over the years—who not only provide excellent services to us but sometimes also our clients, thank you for joining us in the work, and seeing your part in it not just as doing business but joining us in the mission.

To all the area churches—that have supported us, volunteered with us, sponsored our houses and our men, provided inspiration to us, and been filled with people in your pews who were and are passionate about the work of the Kingdom, we are proud to call ourselves fellow soldiers with you.

And to those early churches—you know who you are. You allowed us to cry on your alters during the wilderness and ask for help and simply tell our story. Those were some of the best church services I'll ever be in. Desperation for God brings tears often, but unites His family in ways that nothing else can. Thank you for opening up your doors and services to us. We knew we were kind-of pitiful, but you made us feel valuable. Thank you!

AFTERWORD

Nobody ever knew what caused it. All they knew was that all was lost.

With Mom, Dad, and baby boy asleep in their mobile home, they had no reason to go to bed worried, other than that life was pretty hard and making ends meet a daily challenge. They considered themselves hard working people, but as low-skilled workers they only commanded low-wage incomes.

But they were together. They would keep pressing on.

Then, choked and burning lungs and oppressive heat woke them up. Fire! The mobile home was on fire. The fear was paralyzing. How could this be happening? We must get out!!

When the couple walked into the office of Tim Revis a few days later, they were desperate. They had heard that this man owned a manufactured home dealership but more importantly they had heard that he was kind and generous and helped many people in need.

We are heartbroken, they thought. *How can we get through this without breaking down?*

But they managed it. They told their heartbreaking story to Tim. They had lost everything in the fire, had no money and no insurance, and their baby boy was dead.

Excruciating tears flowed.

Today, Tim Revis, the founder of Homes of Hope, still tells the story with genuine and painful emotion. "Is there anything you can do to help us?", they asked.

What followed was help. Tim helped them out of the resources that he had. But what also followed was a haunting thought. *How many more are desperate like this family?*

Then haunting turned into hope.

Soon after that day, sometime during the middle of the night, Tim was awoken from a dream and heard the words from God that changed destinies. "Homes of Hope". And the idea for the beginning flowed out of that name.

The amazing thing in this story, to me, isn't so much Tim's dream and idea that came out of this family's desperation and hopelessness. It is that out of it, an end to desperation happened for thousands of people who have been touched by Homes of Hope since then, and the beginnings of hope for them too.

So many times we question bad things that happen and some even shake their fists at God for allowing them. But to think about this one single heartbreak stricken family who walked into a man's office in utter desperation, to ask for help, that led to eliminating desperation for so many in the years that followed, is truly amazing.

Bad things happen to good people, yes. But good things happen out of bad things when God intervenes.

Homes of Hope would not exist except for this middle of the night dream, but it would also not exist except for this terrible tragedy and the desperation it produced.

We don't know what happened to that family after Tim helped them, because Homes of Hope did not exist then. There is no case file or record for follow up. But what we do know, is that their story produced the story that you have just read. The story of life change for so many.

The suffering of that one family was terrible and hard, but it was seed for a harvest of hope. Homes of Hope.

Made in the USA
Columbia, SC
23 April 2022